PRESIDENT'S MALARIA INITIATIVE

Tanzania

Malaria Operational Plan FY 2016

TABLE OF CONTENTS

ABBREVIATIONS and ACRONYMS

ACT	Artemisinin-based combination therapy
ADDO	Accredited drug dispensary outlet
AL	Artemether-lumefantrine
ANC	Antenatal care
ASAQ	Artesunate-amodiaquine
BCC	Behavior change communication
BRN	Big Results Now initiative
CBHPP	Community Based Health Program Policy
CD	Continuous distribution (of ITNs)
CDC	Centers for Disease Control and Prevention
CM	Case Management
CHMT	Council Health Management Team
DFID	Department for International Development
DHMT	District Health Management Team
DHS	Demographic and Health Survey
DWL	Durable wall liner
eLMIS	Electronic logistics management information system
EPI	Expanded Program on Immunizations
EUV	End Use Verification
FANC	Focused Antenatal Care
FELTP	Field Epidemiology and Field Training Program
FY	Fiscal year
GHI	Global Health Initiative
Global Fund	Global Fund to Fight AIDS, Tuberculosis and Malaria
GoT	Government of Tanzania
HMIS	Health management information system
HSS	Health systems strengthening
iCCM	Integrated community case management
IDSR	Infectious disease surveillance and response
IPTp	Intermittent preventive treatment in pregnant women
IRS	Indoor residual spraying
ITN	Insecticide-treated mosquito net
LMU	Logistics management unit
MCN	Malaria case notification
M&E	Monitoring and evaluation
MEEDS	Malaria Epidemic Early Detection System
MIP	Malaria in pregnancy
MIS	Malaria Indicator Survey
MNCH	Maternal, newborn and child health
MoHSW	Ministry of Health and Social Welfare
MPR	Malaria Program Review
MOP	Malaria Operational Plan
MSD	Medical Stores Department
NBS	National Bureau of Statistics

NHL	National Health Laboratory
NMCP	National Malaria Control Program
PEPFAR	President's Emergency Plan for AIDS Relief
PHCC	Primary health care centre
PHCU	Primary health care unit
PCV	Peace Corps volunteer
PMI	President's Malaria Initiative
PMO-RALG	Prime Minister's Office-Regional Administration and Local Government
PMTCT	Prevention of mother to child transmission
QA/QC	Quality assurance/quality control
RBF	Results-based financing
RBM	Roll Back Malaria
RCH	Reproductive and child health
RDT	Rapid diagnostic test
RHMT	Regional health management team
SHCC	Shehia health custodian committee
SNP	School net program
SP	Sulfadoxine-pyrimethamine
SPA	Service Provision Assessment
THMIS	Tanzania HIV and Malaria Indicator Survey
TNVS	Tanzania National Voucher Scheme
TWG	Technical Working Group
UCC	Universal Coverage Campaign (of ITNs)
UNICEF	United Nations Children's Fund
USAID	United States Agency for International Development
USG	United States Government
WHO	World Health Organization
ZAMEP	Zanzibar Malaria Elimination Program

I. EXECUTIVE SUMMARY

When it was launched in 2005, the goal of the President's Malaria Initiative (PMI) was to reduce malaria-related mortality by 50% across 15 high-burden countries in sub-Saharan Africa through a rapid scale-up of four proven and highly effective malaria prevention and treatment measures: insecticide-treated mosquito nets (ITNs); indoor residual spraying (IRS); accurate diagnosis and prompt treatment with artemisinin-based combination therapies (ACTs); and intermittent preventive treatment of pregnant women (IPTp). With the passage of the Tom Lantos and Henry J. Hyde Global Leadership against HIV/AIDS, Tuberculosis, and Malaria Act in 2008, PMI developed a U.S. Government Malaria Strategy for 2009–2014. This strategy included a long-term vision for malaria control in which sustained high coverage with malaria prevention and treatment interventions would progressively lead to malaria-free zones in Africa, with the ultimate goal of worldwide malaria eradication by 2040-2050. Consistent with this strategy and the increase in annual appropriations supporting PMI, four new sub-Saharan African countries and one regional program in the Greater Mekong Subregion of Southeast Asia were added in 2011. The contributions of PMI, together with those of other partners, have led to dramatic improvements in the coverage of malaria control interventions in PMI-supported countries, and all 15 original countries have documented substantial declines in all-cause mortality rates among children less than five years of age.

In 2015, PMI launched the next six-year strategy, setting forth a bold and ambitious goal and objectives. The PMI Strategy 2015-2020 takes into account the progress over the past decade and the new challenges that have arisen. Malaria prevention and control remains a major U.S. foreign assistance objective and PMI's Strategy fully aligns with the U.S. Government's vision of ending preventable child and maternal deaths and ending extreme poverty. It is also in line with the goals articulated in the RBM Partnership's second generation global malaria action plan, *Action and Investment to defeat Malaria (AIM) 2016-2030: for a Malaria-Free World* and WHO's updated *Global Technical Strategy: 2016-2030*. Under the PMI Strategy 2015-2020, the U.S. Government's goal is to work with PMI-supported countries and partners to further reduce malaria deaths and substantially decrease malaria morbidity, towards the long-term goal of elimination.

Tanzania was selected as a PMI focus country in FY 2006.

This FY 2016 Malaria Operational Plan presents a detailed implementation plan for Tanzania, based on the strategies of PMI, the National Malaria Control Program (NMCP) strategy, and the Zanzibar Malaria Elimination Program (ZAMEP) strategy. It was developed in consultation with the NMCP, ZAMEP, and with the participation of national and international partners involved in malaria prevention and control in the country. The activities that PMI is proposing to support fit in well with both malaria strategies and plan and build on investments made by PMI and other partners to improve and expand malaria-related services, including the Global Fund to Fight AIDS, Tuberculosis, and Malaria (Global Fund) malaria grants. This document briefly reviews the current status of malaria control policies and interventions in Tanzania, describes progress to date, identifies challenges and unmet needs to achieving the targets of the NMCP and PMI, and provides a description of activities that are planned with FY 2016 funding.

The most recent national-level data for malaria interventions in Tanzania comes from the 2011-12 Tanzania HIV/AIDS-Malaria Indicator Survey (THMIS) and shows further impressive improvements in nearly all malaria indicators when compared with 2005 and 2010 figures. Ninety-one percent of Mainland households owned at least one ITN, with 72% of children under five years of age and 75% of pregnant women sleeping under an ITN. This compares with just 63% ownership and 64% and 57% usage in the 2010 Demographic and Health Survey (DHS). In Zanzibar, ITN ownership and usage fell somewhat when compared with the 2010 DHS; 74% of households now own at least one ITN and estimates of use among children under five years of age and pregnant women are 51% and 36%, respectively. Malaria prevalence in Zanzibar remained extremely low at less than 1% in the 2011-12 THMIS.

The proposed FY 2016 PMI budget for Tanzania is $45 million. PMI will support the following intervention areas with these funds:

Insecticide-treated nets (ITNs): The second ITN universal coverage campaign (UCC) for the Tanzania Mainland, delivering 22 million ITNs to 22 of the 25 regions, began in mid-2015 and will be completed by April 2016. PMI procured ITNs covering two regions, with the remainder procured through Global Fund. As a means of sustaining universal coverage on the Mainland, PMI is supporting a pilot for a school-based ITN distribution program in three regions in the south of the country: Ruvuma, Lindi, and Mtwara. In August 2014, the school-based net program delivered 500,000 ITNs to school children in first, third, fifth, seventh, ninth, and eleventh grades, reaching over 2,300 schools in these regions. A rigorous evaluation, to be completed in mid-2015, will be used to assess the contribution of this approach for maintaining high and equitable coverage. The third school net program (SNP) distribution is planned for August 2015.

The Tanzania National Voucher Scheme (TNVS), which was instrumental in delivering ITNs to pregnant women for over a decade and delivered just under 2 million ITNs in 2013, was ended in June 2014 following the discovery of fraud. It was decided that PMI, in close consultation with the NMCP, Prime Minister's Office Regional Administration and Local Government, and other key Ministry of Health and Social Welfare (MoHSW) personnel, will guide the process of designing and launching a new approach based on free delivery of ITNs to pregnant woman at their first antenatal care (ANC) visit. This new approach will be launched in early 2016.

Zanzibar completed its first UCC in March of 2012, distributing 660,000 ITNs. ZAMEP is planning a second UCC in late 2015 or 2016, depending on availability of funds from Global Fund and other partners, including DFID and PMI. Zanzibar launched a robust continuous delivery program in June 2014 that relies on several channels, including: antenatal care (ANC) delivery to pregnant women, vaccination clinic delivery to children, community-based delivery, and delivery as part of malaria case detection. About 115,000 nets were delivered through these channels in first six months following the launch.

With FY 2016 funding, PMI will procure and support the distribution of about 1,665,000 ITNs through ANC clinics and schools in a total of seven high malaria endemic regions in the Lake Zone and the South. On Zanzibar, PMI will procure and support continuous distribution of about 250,000 ITNs, through ANC, vaccination clinics and community-based channels. Due to uncertainty around a Zanzibar universal coverage campaign, PMI will remain flexible and adapt its approach depending on the level of Global Fund support for a mass campaign.

Indoor residual spraying (IRS): The Mainland reduced the targeted area for IRS from 659,146 structures in 2012/2013, protecting over 3 million people, to about 445,000 structures in 2014 and about 390,000 structures in 2015, protecting about 2 million inhabitants each year. One factor in the reduction in the number of structures sprayed was the switch in 2014 to a more expensive, but longer lasting insecticide, pirimiphos-methyl CS.

In 2014, Zanzibar used focal spraying to cover about 60,000 structures and in 2015 to cover about 65,000 structures, protecting about 300,000 and 340,000 inhabitant, respectively, representing approximately 25% of Zanzibar's population.

For 2016 the projected coverage on the Mainland will be 400,000 structures, protecting about 2 million people; Zanzibar will continue to use focal spraying with a target of 25,000 structures protecting about 125,000 inhabitants. For 2017, using FY 2016 funding, PMI will support targeted IRS in the Lake Zone reaching approximately 350,000 structures protecting 1.5 million people; Zanzibar will use focal spraying of about 20,000 structures, protecting about 100,000 inhabitants. PMI will support spraying in Geita through a public-private partnership with Geita Gold Mine. PMI will supply the insecticide and Geita Gold Mine will pay the operational costs for spraying. Pirimiphos-methyl CS will be used in 2016 for the third consecutive year. PMI, NMCP and partners have recommended a rotation in 2017 to different non-pyrethroid insecticide.

Malaria in pregnancy (MIP): The World Health Organization (WHO) recommends control and prevention of MIP via a three-pronged approach: distribution of ITNs through antenatal care clinics, provision of IPTp with sulfadoxine-pyrimethamine (SP), and prompt case management of pregnant women with malaria. The Mainland implements all three activities; however, due to low prevalence in Zanzibar, the ZAMEP has adopted a policy of screening pregnant women by rapid diagnostic test (RDT) at the first ANC visit and treating those testing positive according to national guidelines.

The IPTp3+ policy was officially adopted by the MoHSW in 2014 and training of staff at public dispensaries, hospitals, and health centers has been completed. In 2015, quality improvement and supervision of MIP service providers is taking place in 88 districts in Kagera and Mara regions and over 400 prevention of mother to child transmission (PMTCT) and reproductive and child health (RCH) clinics in Lindi and Mtwara regions. Quarterly tracking of SP stocks at health facilities and regular feedback meetings with health management teams are also taking place. Phase II of the Safe Motherhood Campaign, designed to improve uptake of all ANC services, is underway with an emphasis on IPTp3+.

With FY 2016 funds, PMI will support continued training and supervision for IPTp3+ and case management (CM) integrated with family planning, maternal and child health, and HIV programming. Behavior change communication (BCC) to boost ITN use, ANC attendance, and IPTp uptake will continue. PMI will support provision of long-lasting ITNs to pregnant women through continuous distribution at ANC on the Mainland and Zanzibar.

Case management: The goal of the Tanzanian malaria control strategy is to achieve and maintain universal access to high quality malaria diagnostic testing and treatment in both public and private health facilities. Since 2006 PMI has supported both Mainland Tanzania and Zanzibar to 1) procure and implement RDT testing in public health facilities, 2) improve the testing performance of both malaria microscopy and RDT via trainings and supportive supervision, 3) disseminate revised diagnosis and treatment guidelines, 4) procure ACTs and artesunate for treatment of severe malaria, and 5) improve supply chain management. In addition PMI funded drug efficacy monitoring to verify that *in vivo* efficacy of ACT remains high.

With FY 2016 funds PMI will procure commodities including mRDT, ACT, and artesunate and will continue to support mRDT and microscopy quality assurance and quality control systems. This latter will include maintenance of a National Slide Bank on the Mainland. PMI will support the NMCP to scale up the introduction of mRDT in accredited drug dispensary outlets (ADDOs) and to support a pilot program of integrated Community Case Management in three districts. To improve case management of febrile illnesses including malaria, PMI will support facility-based provision of health services for improved diagnosis and treatment in the regions that will provide support for technical meetings to develop case management guidance and supporting materials in Zanzibar. PMI will continue to support strengthening of pharmaceutical management and the supply chain system in both Mainland and Zanzibar.

Health systems strengthening and capacity building: PMI and the Government of Tanzania (GoT) aim to bolster the achievement of malaria control results and more importantly to sustain these gains as the country strives towards elimination of malaria. In particular, PMI funds prioritize the following systems strengthening areas: 1) addressing critical health workforce shortages, 2) improving the availability of needed skills in the workforce to lead malaria control efforts, 3) reducing drug stockouts, 4) decreasing donor dependency for financing of malaria, 5) strengthening accountability and management of health care, and 6) improving data for decision-making. PMI support of health systems strengthening in 2006 initially focused on activities closely linked to malaria control, such as information systems strengthening for supply chain, institutional strengthening of planning capabilities of the NMCP and the ZAMEP, and capacity building of the National Bureau of Statistics to conduct major surveys like the DHS, Service Provision Assessment (SPA), and the THMIS. Over the years, PMI broadened its support of systems strengthening to address workforce shortages, and inadequate management and planning of health services and limited resources.

With FY 2016 funds, PMI will be used to support a comprehensive health system strengthening (HSS) activity that will 1) strengthen governance at the national and district levels to use resources transparently, to enable citizen engagement in planning and monitoring, and to produce results in health care, 2) increase domestic resources for health care as well as improve use of funds in terms of effectiveness, efficiency, and obtaining value for money, 3) improve equity in the distribution of health care workers providing quality essential health services, and 4) increase use of available data to inform decision-making processes at both the national and local levels. PMI will also continue to strengthen the supply chain system, including the GoT's ability to better quantify, forecast, budget, monitor and ensure stock availability at the point of service delivery. In addition to continuing these existing activities, PMI will also support two new systems strengthening areas. First, PMI will provide support for Tanzania's government led results-based financing (RBF) activity, by supporting performance payments to facilities for provision of high quality malaria services and to supply chain actors for on time provision of key malaria commodities. Second, PMI will contribute to the GoT-led initiative to create an app that reaches down to the facility to allow for more frequent electronic logistics management information system (eLMIS) reporting. PMI will also continue to support the NMCP and ZAMEP in capacity building activities. PMI contributed to support the two-year Tanzanian Field Epidemiology and Laboratory

Training Program (FELTP). Trainees from this program have participated in various malaria control activities at the NMCP and the ZAMEP, including malaria surveillance and outbreak investigations and most return to the Ministry of Health on completion of their training. In addition, the Peace Corps continues to support BCC and surveillance activities and to effectively engage with their communities to approach malaria education and prevention in innovative ways.

Behavior change communication (BCC): PMI's BCC investments focus on key messaging around testing and treatment with the Not Every Fever is Malaria Campaign, prevention and treatment of malaria in pregnancy with the Safe Motherhood Campaign, the school net program, and the Malaria Safe initiative to engage private companies in promoting malaria prevention and control for their employees and communities. In addition, PMI supports the Community Change Agent platform to directly reach nearly 1 million people with messages on net use and care; adherence to diagnostic testing results and treatment; IRS, and malaria in pregnancy. In Zanzibar, PMI supports ZAMEP's BCC unit to communicate messages on active case detection and response and continuous net distribution.

In FY 2016, BCC efforts will continue to focus on case management, the IPTp3+ roll out, the school net distribution project, IRS, and increased engagement of private companies on the Mainland. BCC efforts through mass media and interpersonal communication will also focus on engaging communities to work together to ensure households are accessing, using and caring for their nets as well as accessing health facilities for testing and treatment and MIP services. Based on malaria stratification, BCC messaging and interventions will be tailored to respond to each region and district's unique situation. In Zanzibar, PMI will continue to support the BCC unit of the ZAMEP and the communication campaigns for continuous distribution of nets and to support the case detection and response teams with messages to promote preventive measures and prompt care-seeking.

Monitoring and evaluation (M&E): Key objectives of the Tanzanian malaria strategy are to achieve and maintain 100% reporting of routine and periodic malaria indicators, to have a well-functioning early epidemic detection system and to strengthen monitoring and evaluation of malaria control activities and strategies. PMI has extensively supported the NMCP and ZAMEP to expand and improve the Health Information Management System (HMIS) and District Health Information Software 2 (DHIS 2), infectious disease surveillance and response (IDSR) systems, routine monitoring systems, the Malaria Epidemic Early Detection System (MEEDS), and malaria case notification (MCN) in Zanzibar. PMI also contributed substantial funding to several nationwide periodic surveys including the DHS which is conducted every 4-5 years, the 2007 and 2011 THMIS, and the SPA carried out in 2006 and 2014. PMI also supports entomologic monitoring and a system of 22 sentinel sites on the Mainland and seven in Zanzibar.

To further epidemic detection and control with FY 2016 funding PMI will support the continuation of the rollout of the electronic Infectious Disease Surveillance and Response (IDSR) system and the maintenance of the MEEDS and outbreak response system in Zanzibar. PMI will also support a routine system strengthening activity to improve malaria data quality and use within the HMIS and will provide funds to the NMCP and ZAMEP to conduct and oversee integrated supportive supervision and to coordinate technical working groups for all malaria interventions. A new Malaria Indicator Survey (MIS) is planned for 2017, which PMI will support in conjunction with other partners. Entomologic monitoring for vector resistance and behavior will continue and will include quality assurance monitoring and PCR-based monitoring.

Operational research (OR): While PMI supports operational research to help guide malaria control activities, neither the NMCP nor the ZAMEP have an official operational research strategy.

The Mainland has engaged in PMI-supported OR activities in past years including the monitoring of parasitemia prevalence among pregnant women and infants in the Lake Zone. This OR activity was supported with FY 2011 funds and completed in December 2013. With core funds, PMI is currently supporting a multi-year, two-arm cluster randomized trial study that aims to assess the protective efficacy of a non-pyrethroid insecticide impregnated durable wall liner (DWL) plus ITNs, vs ITNs alone. The study is on track to begin after the start of the long rainy season in September/October 2015. With FY 2014 funds, PMI is supporting a study to explore the relationship between net damage, remaining insecticide, and feeding inhibition in susceptible and resistant vectors in hut trials. The results will help to define a) the cut-offs to be used to determine "end of useful life" and b) how the cut-offs need to be adjusted with increasing vector resistance.

No new OR activities are proposed with FY 2016 funding.

II. STRATEGY

1. Introduction

When it was launched in 2005, the goal of PMI was to reduce malaria-related mortality by 50% across 15 high-burden countries in sub-Saharan Africa through a rapid scale-up of four proven and highly effective malaria prevention and treatment measures: insecticide-treated mosquito nets (ITNs); indoor residual spraying (IRS); accurate diagnosis and prompt treatment with artemisinin-based combination therapies (ACTs); and intermittent preventive treatment of pregnant women (IPTp). With the passage of the Tom Lantos and Henry J. Hyde Global Leadership against HIV/AIDS, Tuberculosis, and Malaria Act in 2008, PMI developed a U.S. Government Malaria Strategy for 2009–2014. This strategy included a long-term vision for malaria control in which sustained high coverage with malaria prevention and treatment interventions would progressively lead to malaria-free zones in Africa, with the ultimate goal of worldwide malaria eradication by 2040-2050. Consistent with this strategy and the increase in annual appropriations supporting PMI, four new sub-Saharan African countries and one regional program in the Greater Mekong Subregion of Southeast Asia were added in 2011. The contributions of PMI, together with those of other partners, have led to dramatic improvements in the coverage of malaria control interventions in PMI-supported countries, and all 15 original countries have documented substantial declines in all-cause mortality rates among children less than five years of age.

In 2015, PMI launched the next six-year strategy, setting forth a bold and ambitious goal and objectives. The PMI Strategy 2015-2020 takes into account the progress over the past decade and the new challenges that have arisen. Malaria prevention and control remains a major U.S. foreign assistance objective and PMI's Strategy fully aligns with the U.S. Government's vision of ending preventable child and maternal deaths and ending extreme poverty. It is also in line with the goals articulated in the RBM Partnership's second generation global malaria action plan, *Action and Investment to defeat Malaria (AIM) 2016-2030: for a Malaria-Free World* and WHO's updated *Global Technical Strategy: 2016-2030*. Under the PMI Strategy 2015-2020, the U.S. Government's goal is to work with PMI-supported countries and partners to further reduce malaria deaths and substantially decrease malaria morbidity, towards the long-term goal of elimination.

Tanzania was selected as a PMI focus country in FY 2006.

This FY 2016 Malaria Operational Plan presents a detailed implementation plan for Tanzania, based on the strategies of PMI, the National Malaria Control Program (NMCP) strategy, and the Zanzibar Malaria Elimination Program (ZAMEP) strategy. It was developed in consultation with the NMCP, ZAMEP, and with the participation of national and international partners involved in malaria prevention and control in the country. The activities that PMI is proposing to support fit in well with both malaria strategies and plans and builds on investments made by PMI and other partners to improve and expand malaria-related services, including the Global Fund to Fight AIDS, Tuberculosis, and Malaria (Global Fund) malaria grants. This document briefly reviews the current status of malaria control policies and interventions in Tanzania, describes progress to date, identifies challenges and unmet needs to achieving the targets of the NMCP and PMI, and provides a description of activities that are planned with FY 2016 funding.

2. Malaria situation in Tanzania

Ninety-three percent of the population on the Mainland and the entire population of Zanzibar live in areas where malaria is transmitted. Unstable seasonal malaria transmission occurs in approximately 20% of the country, while stable malaria with seasonal variation occurs in another 20%. The remaining malaria endemic areas in Tanzania (60%) are characterized as stable perennial transmission. *Plasmodium falciparum* accounts for 96% of malaria infection in Tanzania, with the remaining 4% due to *P. malariae* and *P. ovale*.

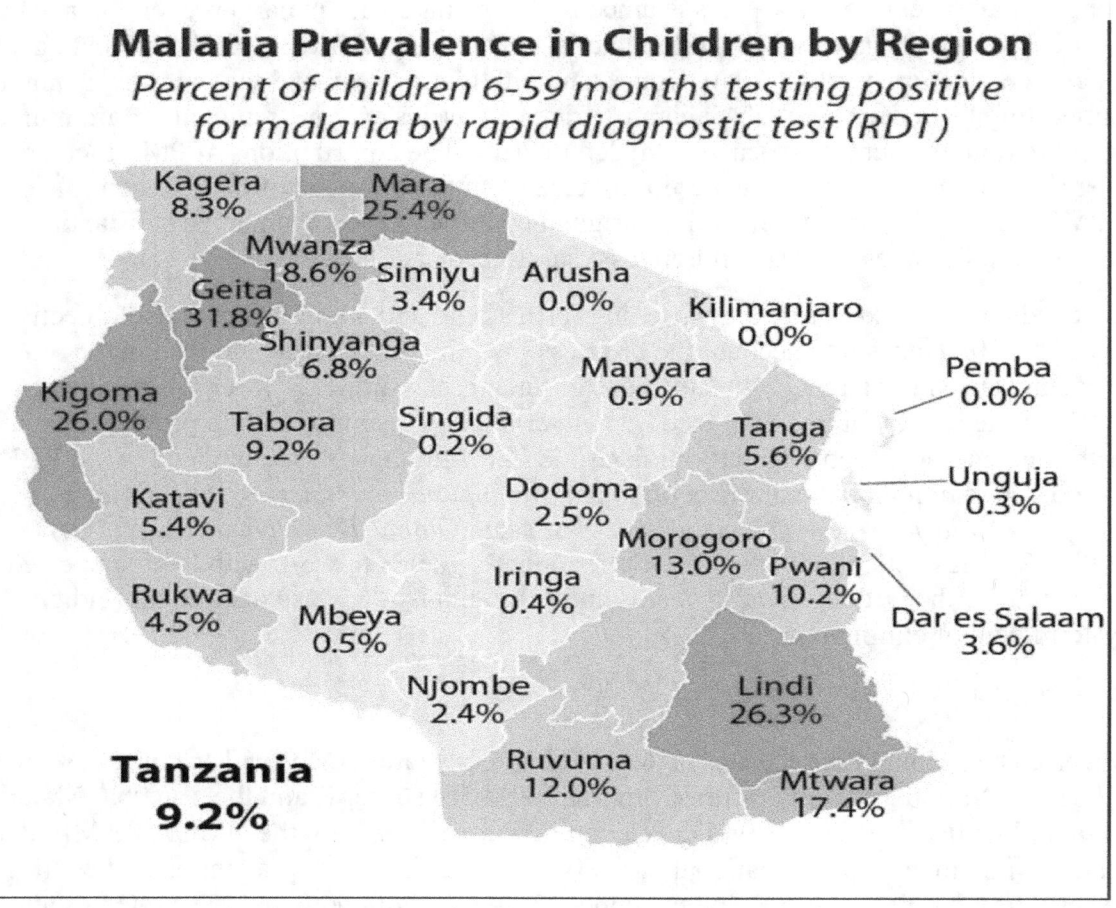

Source: 2011-2012 Tanzania HIV and Malaria Indicator Survey (THMIS)

The principal vectors of malaria in Tanzania are mosquitoes of the *Anopheles gambiae* complex (*An. gambiae s.s.* and *An. arabiensis*), with *An. arabiensis* increasing to 78% of the vector population in sentinel site collections in 2014. *An. funestus* is prevalent on the Mainland as well, particularly in Kagera Region. In Zanzibar, high coverage of ITNs and IRS has resulted in a shift in the malaria vector population from *An. gambiae* to nearly 100% *An. arabiensis* as of 2014. *An. funestus* has been on the rise in parts of Pemba since 2011, constituting a large proportion of outdoor biting and resting collections in 2013-2014.

The 2011–2012 Tanzania HIV/AIDS Malaria Indicator Survey (THMIS) showed that 9% of Mainland children under five years of age had tested positive for malaria, down from 18% in the 2007-08 THMIS. Prevalence varied by region variation from <1% in the highlands of Arusha to 26% along the Lake Victoria shores (figure above). The same survey showed a much lower malaria prevalence of 0.2% in Zanzibar. On the Mainland, more than 32% of all outpatient attendances are attributable to malaria, resulting in an estimated 7.3 million both confirmed and clinical malaria cases annually, 3.4 and 3.9 million cases for under five and above five years of age respectively. According to the World Malaria Report (2014), 8,526 malaria deaths are reported annually in the Mainland among all age groups.

Tanzania registered a 45% reduction in all-cause under-five mortality from 146/1000 live births in 1999 to 81/1000 live births in 2010.

Infant and Under-five Mortality Rates for Five-year Periods Preceding Nationwide Household Surveys, Tanzania				
	1999 **DHS**	**2004-05** **DHS**	**2007-08** **THMIS**	**2009-10** **DHS**
Infant mortality rate (95% C.I.)	99.1 (85-113)	68.0 (61-75)	57.7 (50-65)	51 (44-57)
Under-five mortality rate (95% C.I.)	146.6 (128-165)	112.0 (103-122)	91.4 (83-100)	81 (72-90)

The trend analysis of 1999 -2012 demographic surveys shows that the decline was greater in rural areas compared to urban areas, and more in medium to high malaria risk areas, indicating that interventions are reaching the poor and the more at-risk populations (January 2012 Roll Back Malaria report *Progress and Impact series: Focus on Mainland Tanzania*; June 2012 *Evaluation of the Impact of Malaria Interventions on Mortality in Children in Mainland Tanzania* available at http://www.pmi.gov/docs/default-source/default-document-library/tools-curricula/tanzania_ie_report.pdf).

3. **Country health system delivery structure and Ministry of Health (MoH) organization**

Two separate Ministries of Health operate in the United Republic of Tanzania, one for the Mainland and one for Zanzibar. Each Ministry has its own malaria control program and malaria strategic plan. The

National Malaria Control Program (NMCP) serves the Mainland, while the Zanzibar Malaria Elimination Program (ZAMEP) serves Zanzibar.

The Mainland's NMCP has established several committees to coordinate and direct national malaria control policies and priorities. The National Malaria Steering Committee is the body that is expected to provide strategic and policy direction for malaria activities on the Mainland. It is to be chaired by the Chief Medical Officer and will include representatives from leading stakeholders. The ITN strategies and policies are coordinated through the National Insecticide-Treated Nets Program. A diagnostics and case management working group guides NMCP policies/strategies for strengthening and expanding malaria case management. Surveillance, monitoring and evaluation (SM&E) and behavior change communication (BCC) technical working groups (TWGs) are also active. PMI is represented on each of the technical working groups.

The Zanzibar Malaria Elimination Program provides leadership for malaria activities on Zanzibar. ZAMEP has Technical Working Groups for all major intervention areas, i.e. vector control, case management and diagnosis, BCC and SM&E, the working groups are expected to be fully operationalised before end of 2015. PMI is expecting to be represented on these technical working groups. PMI is also supporting the establishment of a Technical Advisory Group, comprised of both local and international experts, to help guide ZAMEP's pre-elimination activities. It is expected that this group will be convened in late 2015.

The GoT operates a decentralized health system, organized around three functional levels: council (primary level), regional (secondary level), and referral hospitals (tertiary level). Within the framework of the ongoing local government reforms, regional and councils have full responsibilities for delivering health services within their areas of jurisdiction, and report administratively to the Prime Minister's Office – Regional Administration and Local Government (PMO-RALG).

Under this system, the councils have full mandate for planning, implementation, monitoring and evaluation of health services. Each council has a District Medical Officer who heads the Council Health Management Team (CHMT) and is answerable to the District Executive Director, the head of the council. CHMTs are responsible for provision of services in dispensaries, health centers and district or District Designated Hospitals.

The Regional Health Management Teams (RHMTs) are responsible for interpreting health policies at the regional level. The Ministry of Health and Social Welfare (MoHSW) is responsible for policy formulation, supervision and regulation for all health services throughout the country, as well as playing a direct role in the management of tertiary health services.

In the Zanzibar Ministry of Health, the Minister and his Deputy provide policy direction for health service delivery that is executed through the offices of the Principal Secretary and the Director General for Medical Services. At the central level four directorates have been established to support specific Ministry of Health departments/Units/Sections and Programmes, .i.e. Planning, Policy and Research; Administration and Personnel; Curative Services; and the Directorate for Preventive Services and Health Promotion which includes the Zanzibar Malaria Elimination Programme.

Health service delivery in Zanzibar is through a hierarchy of health facilities categorized into public, private and government institutional health facilities managed by military and defense forces. This system allows for a chain of referrals from a basic primary health care facility to the referral hospital. This is characterized by three levels: primary (Primary Health Care Units and Primary Health Care Centres), secondary (District Hospitals), and tertiary (Mnazi Mmoja and other specialized hospitals).

There are 134 Primary Health Care Units (PHCU); 34 are categorised as PHCU+ that provide additional services such as dental, pharmacy, delivery and laboratory services, four (4) are Primary Health Care Centres (PHCCs) that provide all the services of the PHCU+ with the additional of inpatient care and X-ray; three (3) are district hospitals - located in Pemba that provide second –line referral services.

ZAMEP is supporting districts through Zonal Health Management Teams. There are two zones in Zanzibar and each has its District Health Management Team (DHMT) headed by a District Medical Officer who is overall in charge of health, including malaria. The DHMTs monitor the malaria situation in the villages (*shehias*) on monthly and quarterly basis through Shehia Health Custodian Committees (SHCC). Most *shehias* have SHCC that are functional. The SHCC acts as the advisory board for all health affairs in their locality. The committee collaborates with health workers in planning and implementation of malaria services delivered to the community.

Distribution of health facilities in Mainland Tanzania					
Facility type	Public	Parastatal	FBOs	Private	Total
Hospital	112	9	111	33	264
Health Center	467	19	139	59	684
Dispensary	3,990	192	597	790	5,607
Total	**4,569**	**220**	**847**	**882**	**6,518**

Source: MoHSW 2013

There are about 6,518 health facilities, of which 70% are owned by the public sector (MoHSW 2013). The system is in the form of a pyramid: on top are specialized hospitals owned by the Ministry and at the bottom are primary health care facilities. Almost 85% of the population gets their health services from primary health care facilities (MoHSW 2013); however, these facilities face a lot of challenges in delivering services including poor infrastructure, shortage of skilled staff and essential medicines.

4. National malaria control strategy

Two separate Ministries of Health operate in the United Republic of Tanzania, one for the Mainland and one for Zanzibar. Each Ministry has its own malaria control program, with separate leadership/management and malaria strategic plans. The NMCP serves only the Mainland, while the Zanzibar Program serves Zanzibar. In 2014 the Zanzibar Malaria Program changed its name to the Zanzibar Malaria Elimination Program (ZAMEP).

Mainland

Under the leadership of a program manager, the NMCP is organized into five cells: case management; vector control; ITNs; information and education; and surveillance, monitoring and evaluation (including operations research). Each cell consists of a team leader and two to four staff members. ZAMEP has similar organizational units and a comparable staff.

The Mainland's NMCP has established several committees to coordinate and direct national malaria control policies and priorities. The Malaria Control Steering Committee is the body that is expected to provide strategic and policy direction for malaria control on the Mainland. It will be chaired by the Chief Medical Officer and will include representatives from leading stakeholders. The organization of this steering committee has been outlined in the new Strategic Plan but has not yet convened. The ITN strategies and policies are coordinated through the National Insecticide Treated Nets Program. A diagnostics and case management technical working group guides NMCP policies/strategies for strengthening and expanding malaria case management. A surveillance and monitoring and evaluation (SM&E) technical working group was re-formed in 2014. PMI is represented on each of these working groups.

The NMCP strategic plan for 2014-2020 includes the following goals:

- To reduce malaria morbidity and malaria deaths by 80% from the 2012 levels by 2020
- To reduce malaria prevalence from 10% in 2012 to 5% in 2016 and to 1% in 2020
- To increase the proportion of women receiving two or more doses of SP during their pregnancy from 32% in 2012 to 80% by 2016

To implement the new strategic plan the NMCP will address the thematic areas of 1) malaria case management, 2) integrated malaria vector control, 3) supportive interventions, such as BCC and monitoring and evaluation (M&E), and 4) program management. Each thematic area has objectives and strategies that support the overarching program goals.

Malaria Case Management

The principal objectives of malaria case management are to minimize severity and complications from malaria infections and thus reduce morbidity/mortality among vulnerable populations and to ensure that all people with malaria have access to appropriate, timely diagnosis and prompt treatment.

Integrated Malaria Vector Control

The objectives of integrated vector control are: 1) to achieve and maintain universal access of ITNs in order to have at least 80% appropriate use by 2020, 2) to consolidate the scope of IRS intervention to protect at least 85% of the population living in areas selected using evidence-based criteria, 3) to scale-up larviciding interventions by 2020 to selected (urban) areas where breeding sites are few, fixed, and findable, and 4) to promote effective environmental management for malaria control among at least 80% of communities through local government authorities (LGAs) in all districts.

Supportive interventions

The main objectives are: 1) improve BCC so that by 2020, 80% of all population at risk of malaria will be aware of the appropriate use of malaria prevention and treatment interventions, 2) to attain 100% reporting of routine and periodic key malaria indicators from all districts, 3) to strengthen malaria surveillance to detect 100% of malaria epidemics within one week of onset, 4) to effectively manage malaria epidemics within two weeks of detection, and 5) to strengthen monitoring and evaluation of malaria control interventions, activities, policies and strategies.

Program Management

The principal objective is to strengthen capacity in program management, resource mobilization and coordination at all levels.

Zanzibar

The ZAMEP's 2013-2018 Strategic Plan focuses on pre-elimination and its vision that by 2018 Zanzibar will have no locally-acquired malaria cases. The ZAMEP expects to achieve this by providing quality, affordable, and cost effective antimalarial interventions and malaria curative services to all people in Zanzibar and by maintaining and expanding a well-performing epidemic detection and response system. The operational objectives in the ZAMEP Strategic Plan are:

- To test 100% of suspected malaria cases with a parasitologic test by 2015 and to provide effective antimalarial treatment to all confirmed cases
- To add primaquine to the treatment regimen by 2017 to reduce gametocytemia levels in the population and thereby limit transmission
- To achieve and maintain 100% coverage with appropriate prevention measures by 2017
- To expand malaria surveillance, conduct reactive case detection and investigate 100% of confirmed malaria cases by 2018
- To establish functional coordination structures for malaria elimination at national, district and *shehia* (village) levels by 2018
- To conduct relevant operational research to evaluate and optimize ongoing activities and monitor resistance to antimalarials and insecticides

5. Updates in the strategy section

As part of the Tanzania Government's effort to transition the country from low to middle-income economy, in February 2015, Tanzanian President Jakaya Kikwete unveiled the Big Results Now (BRN) initiative, modeled on the Malaysian development strategy. A comprehensive system of implementation will focus on six priority areas of the economy: 1) energy and natural gas, 2) agriculture, 3) water, 4) education, 5) transport, and 6) mobilization of resources.[1]The BRN initiative aims at adopting new methods of working under a specified timeframe for delivery of the step-change required. The health sector was added after the initial announcement and the intention is to implement four priorities: 1) equal distribution of skilled health workers from the lower level of primary health care, 2) improved quality of services, 3) availability of important drugs and health equipment, and 4) strengthening reproductive health of mother and child by reducing at least 60% of mortality rate by the year 2018.[2]

---

[1]http://www.pmoralg.go.tz/quick-menu/brn/

[2]http://www.pesatimes.co.tz/news/governance/-big-results-now--initiative-targets-health-sector/tanzania

The health component of BRN builds on Tanzania's Sharpened One Plan and the Reproductive, Maternal, Newborn and Child Health (RMNCH) Scorecard launched by President Kikwete, 15 May 2014.[3]

The Sharpened One Plan aims to:
- Address the unmet need for family planning
- Address the gaps for coverage and quality of care at birth
- Continue the progress already achieved in child health

Based on the data, this plan also advocates for a particular focus on women from the Western and Lake Zones who are being underserved in terms of family planning services, and on rural, poor women and newborns who are not receiving adequate care at birth.[4] The map below shows the regions adopted by the BRN for health interventions. These include many of the highest malaria endemic regions in the country. Overarching health programs, such as results-based financing (RBF) and health system strengthening (HSS), USAID, including PMI, will support work across these three key intervention areas in all regions except for Singida and Katavi.

---

[3]http://www.afro.who.int/en/tanzania/press-materials/item/6565-the-united-republic-of-tanzania-launches-the-sharpened-one-plan-and-the-rmnch-score-card-to-prevent-maternal-newborn-and-child-mortality.html
[4] http://www.mamaye.or.tz/en/evidence/sharpened-one-plan-2014-2015

Figure I: Planned activities for Big Results Now regions

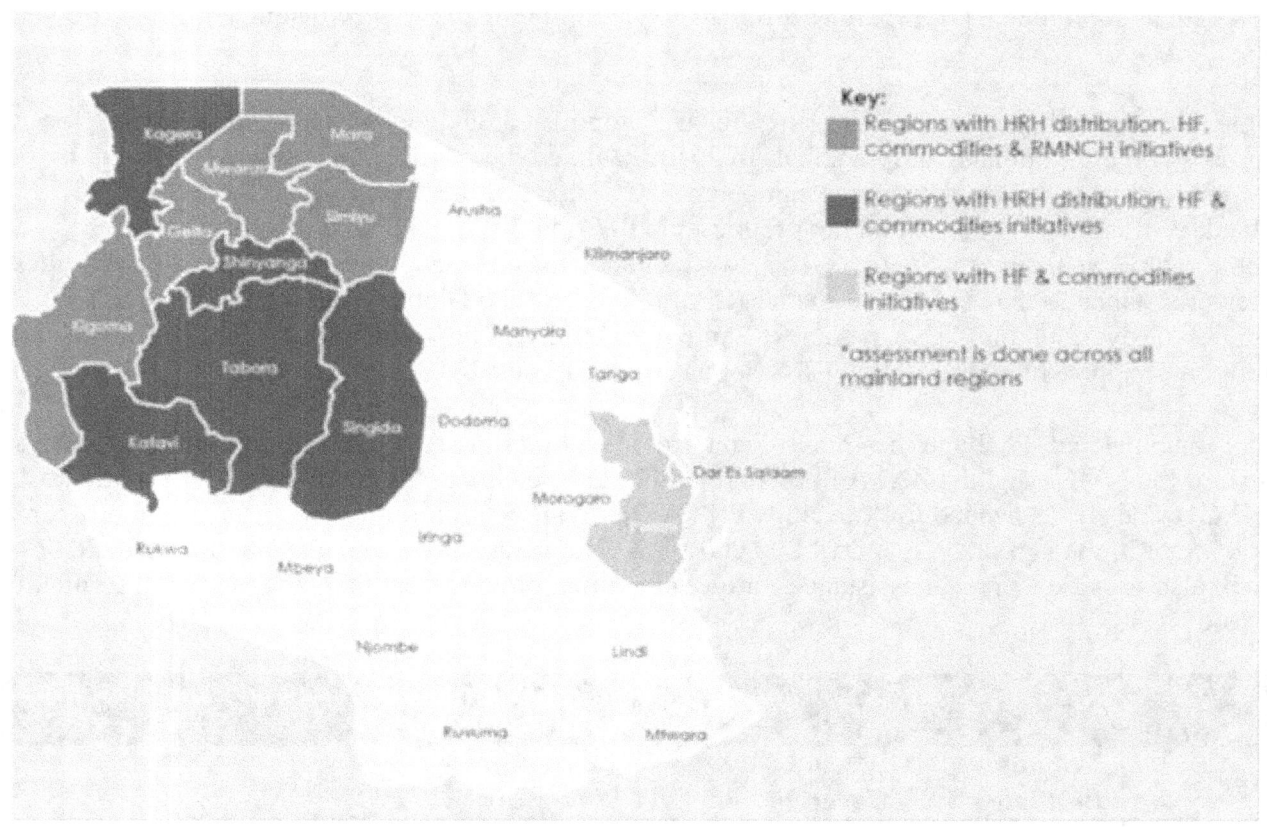

6. Integration, collaboration, and coordination

Funding and Integration with Key Development Partners

The Global Fund and PMI provide more than 90% of malaria funding to mainland Tanzania. Ninety-nine percent of the total malaria control budget in Zanzibar comes from external resources[5], with PMI contributing the largest amount followed by the Global Fund. This does not take into account staff salaries, which are paid by the government. Other donors include WHO, United Nation's Children's Fund (UNICEF), African Development Bank, Japan International Cooperation Agency , Danida, the United Kingdom's Department for International Development (DFID), and research institutions.

Under the Global Fund New Funding Model, the proposed malaria funding level for Tanzania Mainland is $202 million for the 2013-2016 allocation period.[6] Of this, $17 million was earmarked by the Global Fund to be part of pooled funds to support the health system strengthening component of Tanzania's overall grant. Thus, the actual level of funding for malaria is $185 million. A large proportion of these

---

[5] Zanzibar Malaria Strategic Plan 11 (2013-2018)

[6] http://www.theglobalfund.org/en/fundingmodel/allocationprocess/allocations/

funds were already approved in earlier grants, which included funds for an ITN universal coverage campaign and for prompt and effective treatment of malaria cases and detection and containment of malaria epidemics. The NMCP will develop and submit a concept note for the use of these funds in July 2015. Zanzibar submitted a concept note for nearly $11 million in 2014, to be disbursed from 2015 – 2017.

PMI, the Global Fund, and the Swiss Agency for Development and Cooperation provide funding for the ITN strategy on the Mainland and Zanzibar. In 2015, PMI and the Global Fund are jointly providing funds to undertake a universal coverage campaign (UCC) in 22 of the 25 regions in the Tanzania Mainland. PMI is funding the school net program in 2016 and 2017 and PMI will support ANC distribution of ITNs beginning in 2016. The Swiss Agency for Development and Cooperation provides technical assistance to the ITN unit of the NMCP. In Zanzibar, the Global Fund is supporting mass distribution of over 500,000 ITNs in August-September 2015 and PMI will support continuous distribution of approximately 250,000 ITNs annually in 2016 and 2017.

For case management, PMI and the Global Fund provide all funding for ACTs and rapid diagnostic tests (RDTs) for the NMCP and the ZAMEP. In 2016 and 2017, the Global Fund will provide procure most of the ACTs and RDTs needed for Tanzania. PMI will provide $1 million for ACTs and $900,000 for RDTs to help fill the gap in 2016 and $4,800,000 for ACTs, parenteral artesunate, and RDTs in 2017. PMI will also provide technical assistance for quantification, procurement planning, and monitoring of ACTs and RDTs.

Major non-PMI External Sources of Funding for Malaria Control Mainland and Zanzibar, 2014-present			
Source	Amount (millions)	Period Covered	What is covered
Global Fund New Funding Model (Mainland)	$83	January 2016 - December 2017	Sustaining universal ITN coverage with continuous distribution channels, improved malaria case management through the use of RDTs and ACTs in the public and private sectors and improved quality of care in children with severe malaria, M&E
Global Fund New Funding Model (Zanzibar)	$11	January 2015 – December 2017	Supporting mass ITN distribution campaign and sustaining universal coverage with continuous distribution channels, improved malaria case management through the use of RDTs and ACTs in the public and private sectors, BCC, supply chain strengthening and drug quality monitoring HMIS strengthening.
DFID	$36	2014 (cut short; was to run through 2016)	Funding for the Tanzanian National Voucher scheme
Swiss Agency for Development & Cooperation	$6	2013 – 2017	Technical Assistance to ITN and Case Management cells within NMCP

Private Sector

Through the Global Fund, the Clinton Foundation has provided technical assistance to the NMCP and the ZAMEP to introduce ACT and RDTs in the private sector. In 2016 and 2017, PMI will provide funding for the scale-up of this successful program. Beginning in FY 2012, PMI partnered with Geita Gold Mine to spray houses in Geita District. Geita Gold Mine provided funds to the local government for operational costs and PMI is providing the insecticide and technical expertise for microplanning, environmental compliance, data management and reporting, and final disposal of chemical waste. In 2014, the partnership facilitated IRS in the urban and peri-urban wards of Kalangalala and Mtakuja in Geita District, Geita Region.

Malaria Safe is a project that encourages private sector participation in malaria education, prevention, and advocacy. In Tanzania, 52 companies have joined to support activities including sponsorship of World Malaria Day and provision of long-lasting ITNs and case management services to employees. With FY 2015 funds, PMI is supporting outreach to other companies using a PMI-partner designed dashboard that demonstrates the costs associated with malaria and savings associated with malaria prevention. In 2017, PMI will continue to engage Malaria Safe companies in the fight against malaria by supporting the secretariat and coordination meetings, the ministerial steering committee, and expansion of the program to include new companies.

Collaboration with Other USG Programs

PMI works in collaboration with the President's Emergency Plan for AIDS Relief (PEPFAR) on many cross-cutting programmatic issues related to HIV/AIDS and malaria interventions. This has included co-funding two *Tanzania HIV/AIDS and Malaria Indicator Surveys* (THMIS) in 2007 and 2011; co-funding a two-year surveillance officer position in Zanzibar that assisted both the ZAMEP and Zanzibar AIDS Control Program to strengthen surveillance activities and help coordinate disease cluster investigations (FY 2011-2012); and co-funding, since 2007, the Tanzania Field Epidemiology & Laboratory Training Program (FELTP). PMI's support for strengthening malaria diagnostics uses the infrastructure and equipment supplied by PEPFAR. The alignment of PEPFAR and malaria diagnostics activities has avoided duplication of efforts and facilitated the mutual interest in developing and implementing appropriate laboratory quality assurance/quality control (QA/QC) programs.

PMI also partnered with the Department of Defense Walter Reed Army Institute of Research to strengthen the NMCP and the ZAMEP malaria diagnostics QA/QC system. In addition, PMI supports Peace Corps volunteers to develop their capacities for malaria control and promote behavior change communication activities aimed at improving use of ITNs and promotion of early health seeking behavior.

7. PMI goal, objectives, strategic areas, and key indicators

Under the PMI Strategy for 2015-2020, the U.S. Government's goal is to work with PMI-supported countries and partners to further reduce malaria deaths and substantially decrease malaria morbidity, towards the long-term goal of elimination. Building upon the progress to date in PMI-supported countries, PMI will work with NMCPs and partners to accomplish the following objectives by 2020:

1. Reduce malaria mortality by one-third from 2015 levels in PMI-supported countries, achieving over an 80% reduction from PMI's original 2000 baseline levels

2. Reduce malaria morbidity in PMI-supported countries by 40% from 2015 levels

3. Assist at least five PMI-supported countries to meet the World Health Organization's criteria for national or sub-national pre-elimination.[7]

These objectives will be accomplished by emphasizing five core areas of strategic focus:
1. Achieving and sustaining scale of proven interventions
2. Adapting to changing epidemiology and incorporating new tools
3. Improving countries' capacity to collect and use information
4. Mitigating risk against the current malaria control gains
5. Building capacity and health systems towards full country ownership

To track progress toward achieving and sustaining scale of proven interventions (area of strategic focus #1), PMI will continue to track the key indicators recommended by the Roll Back Malaria Monitoring and Evaluation Reference Group as listed below:

- Proportion of households with at least one ITN
- Proportion of households with at least one ITN for every two people
- Proportion of children under five years old who slept under an ITN the previous night
- Proportion of pregnant women who slept under an ITN the previous night
- Proportion of households in targeted districts protected by IRS
- Proportion of children under five years old with fever in the last two weeks for whom advice or treatment was sought
- Proportion of children under five with fever in the last two weeks who had a finger or heel stick
- Proportion receiving an ACT among children under five years old with fever in the last two weeks who received any antimalarial drugs
- Proportion of women who received two or more doses of IPTp for malaria during ANC visits during their last pregnancy

8. Progress on coverage/impact indicators to date

Four nationally representative population-based household surveys and other data sources provide intervention coverage estimates for key malaria outcome indicators between 2004 and 2012. The table below describes current estimates of intervention coverage and impact indicators, respectively, for the Mainland and Zanzibar. The 2004-05 Tanzania Demographic and Health Survey (DHS) provides baseline estimates for the main PMI indicators of interest.

The 2011-12 THMIS collected data on knowledge and behavior regarding HIV/AIDS and malaria and measured HIV prevalence among adults aged 15-49 and malaria parasitemia among children aged 6-59

---

[7] http://whqlibdoc.who.int/publications/2007/9789241596084_eng.pdf

months. It also updated estimates of selected demographic and health indicators covered in previous surveys to more accurately measure trends in malaria infection.

Table I: Evolution of Key Malaria Indicators in Tanzania from 2004/05 to 2011/12

Coverage Indicator	Mainland				Zanzibar			
	2004-05 DHS (%)	2007-08 MIS (%)	2009-10 DHS (%)	2011-12 MIS (%)	2004-05 DHS (%)	2007-08 MIS (%)	2009-10 DHS (%)	2011-12 MIS (%)
Households with at least one ITN	23	38	63	91	28	72	76	74
Children under five years old who slept under an ITN the previous night	16	25	64	73	22	59	55	51
Pregnant women who slept under an ITN the previous night	15	26	57	76	20	51	50	36
Women who received two or more doses of IPTp at ANC visits during their last pregnancy	22	30	27	33	14	52	47	48
Children under five years old with fever in last two weeks who received any antimalarial treatment	58	57	60	55	61	66	17	1.7
Children under five years old with fever in the last two weeks who received treatment with ACTs within 24 hours of onset fever	-	14	27	21	-	9	4	1
Targeted houses adequately sprayed with a residual insecticide in the last 12 months	-	-	95	-	-	94	96	87

Impact Indicators								
	Mainland				Zanzibar			
Impact Indicator	2004-05 DHS	2007-08 MIS	2000-10 DHS	2011-12 MIS	2004-05 DHS	2007-08 MIS	2009-10 DHS	2011-12 MIS
All-cause under-five mortality rate	112	92	81	-	101	79	73	-
Parasitemia prevalence (6-59 mo. old)	-	18.1%	-	9%	-	0.8%	-	0.2%
Anemia (Hb<8 g/dL) prevalence (6-59 mo. old)	11.1%	7.8%	5.5%	5.6%	6.4%	4.7%	3.8%	4.1%

In 2012, the Roll Back Malaria (RBM) Partnership released the results of an Impact Evaluation for Mainland Tanzania that concluded that the lives of an estimated 63,000 children under five have been saved by malaria control interventions since 1999 (January 2012 Roll Back Malaria report of *Progress and Impact series: Focus on Mainland Tanzania*) Zanzibar is currently conducting an Impact Evaluation which should be available in 2015.

9. Other relevant evidence on progress

N/A

10. Challenges and opportunities

One of the major programmatic challenges to malaria prevention and control in Mainland Tanzania is related to human resource constraints, including staff shortages, a lack of adequately trained malaria officers at the regional and district levels, and the very high turnover rate of Ministry of Health staff, particularly in more peripheral settings. In addition, the weak supply chain management system further jeopardizes the ability of the Ministry of Health and the NMCP to deliver malaria prevention and treatment interventions to all health facilities across the Mainland. Finally, weak information systems hamper the ability of the NMCP to monitor malaria control activities and measure progress. PMI is contributing to cross-cutting USAID health systems strengthening (HSS) programs to address some of these problems; however, it is likely to take several years before progress becomes apparent.

In Zanzibar, one of the major programmatic challenges is how to realign activities as the ZAMEP moves towards pre-elimination. Much of the technical information and assistance from the global community focuses on malaria control and prevention and very little is known about how to realign, intensify, or scale-back interventions as regions move toward pre-elimination and elimination. On the other hand, Zanzibar is in the unique position of often being on the cutting edge of activities such as surveillance and case detection. Zanzibar is conducting a number of operational research activities funded by various donors to try and address questions related to pre-elimination. PMI is supporting the establishment of a technical advisory group, comprised of both local and international experts, to help guide ZAMEP's pre-elimination activities.

III. OPERATIONAL PLAN

Through GHI and PMI, the United States Government (USG) is committed to working closely with host governments and within existing national malaria control plans. Efforts are coordinated with other national and international partners, including the Global Fund, RBM, and the non-governmental and private sectors, to ensure that investments are complementary and that RBM and Millennium Development Goals are achieved.

PMI collaborates and coordinates with the NMCP, ZAMEP, and other partners based upon the NMCP's and ZAMEP's strategic goals and priorities. The level of support for each of the interventions takes into consideration the contributions from other donors such as the Government of Tanzania, Global Fund, DFID, and other stakeholders to ensure priority interventions are scaled up to fill gaps, avoid duplication, and target interventions to address regional variations in malaria epidemiology and progress to date.

Mainland Tanzania's goal is malaria control and prevention, focusing certain interventions on areas with the highest transmission and others on routine malaria prevention. For instance, IRS is supported in the Lake Zone, the area with the highest transmission, while ITNs are universally distributed throughout the Mainland. PMI supports all interventions in the NMCP strategic plan except for environmental management and larviciding.

In Zanzibar, decreasing malaria prevalence has prompted the ZAMEP to adopt a new malaria 2013-2018 Strategic Plan, which focuses on achieving pre-elimination by 2018. Zanzibar is re-evaluating its interventions to match the current epidemiology and PMI is supporting these changes. For instance, the ZAMEP is scaling down IRS from blanket to focused spraying and conducting reactive case detection as part of its surveillance program. PMI is supporting the ZAMEP to realign its interventions and is working with the program to ensure rational strategies are adopted that relate to the changing epidemiology. PMI supports all aspects of the ZAMEP strategic plan, except for environmental management and larviciding.

1. Insecticide-treated nets

NMCP/ZAMEP/PMI objectives

Mainland

The NMCP's strategic objective for Integrated Malaria Vector Control for 2014-2020, as presented in the Tanzania National Malaria Strategic Plan: 2014-2020, is to increase the percentage of the population who slept under a long-lasting ITN last night or in a dwelling sprayed with IRS in the past six months from a baseline of 73% in 2012 to 90% in 2020. The specific objective for nets is to maintain universal access to long-lasting ITNs in all transmission settings and control stages, increasing the percentage of households with at least one long-lasting ITN for every two persons from a baseline of 74% in 2012 to 85% in 2020. Specific population targets for net use increase are: 1) all household residents from 67% in 2012 to 80% in 2020, 2) children under five years of age from 71% to 85%, and 3) pregnant women from 73% to 85%.

The Tanzania National Malaria Strategic Plan: 2014-2020 calls for a national universal coverage campaign (UCC) to bring coverage levels to 80% with access to an ITN (as defined as one ITN for every two persons) and continuous distribution to maintain high levels after the mass campaign. Continuous distribution channels include targeted distribution to women through ANC clinics and children at vaccination clinics. Prior to June 2014 this was accomplished through the Tanzania National Voucher Scheme (TNVS).

A modeling exercise indicated that the most appropriate approach to maintain 80% coverage following a universal coverage campaign is a combination of delivery at ANC and vaccination clinics, plus an annual school-based distribution to alternate grades beginning with first grade through eleventh grade (Standards 1,3,5,7 and Forms 2 and 4). The school net program (SNP) is intended to function as an effective distribution mechanism for getting nets into households with at least one school-age child. The combination of ANC, Expanded Program on Immunizations (EPI), and the SNP would potentially reach just over 70% of Tanzanian households, representing about 85% of the population. This assumes that all pregnant women, infants under one and households with a child in school received an ITN from the program.[8] Based on these projections, the NMCP, with support from PMI, Global Fund and Swiss Tropical and Public Health Institute, implemented a school-based distribution pilot in three regions in the south of the country. The second round of the SNP was completed in August 2014 and is being evaluated. Based on the findings, this approach may be adopted and scaled up nationally.

Modeling also showed that to maintain 80% coverage for a ten-year period following a UCC requires an average annual input of 7 million ITNs. The model assumed that ITNs have a three year useful life, i.e. 50% of ITNs are still viable after three years of use in the field. The annual ITN input needed in the first two years following a then proposed 2012 campaign was calculated to be 3.5 and 5.1 million respectively, and rise to near 9 million ITNs annually in later years. [9]

Zanzibar

In the Zanzibar Malaria Strategic Plan III 2013 – 2018, the ZAMEP adopted the WHO definition of universal coverage as one ITN per two people. ITN targets outlined in the Zanzibar malaria strategic plan include increasing access to long-lasting ITNs (i.e. the proportion of individuals living with a ratio of one ITN for every two persons) from a baseline for 35% in 2012 to 100% in 2014 and beyond; increasing use of long-lasting ITNs among pregnant women from 32% in 2012 to 95% in 2017; and increasing use among children under five years of age from 35% in 2012 to 95% in 2016 and beyond. This will be achieved through a combination of UCCs, which are called for every three years, and continuous delivery through facility-based and community-based approaches. At the facility level, free provision of nets to pregnant women at ANC clinic visits was adopted in 2004 and delivery at vaccination clinics was added to the strategy in 2006. Although adopted much earlier, these continuous distribution approaches were launched in June 2014, along with a community distribution approach. This channel delivers ITNs to those in need, including households with no nets, those with unusable or lost nets, those with an uncovered sleeping space, and others. A village committee, led by the village chief (*sheha*), determines who meets the criteria and issues a coupon that can be redeemed for an ITN at

---

[8] Koenker HM, Yukich JO Mkindi A et al. 2013. Analysing and recommending options for maintaining universal coverage with long-lasting insecticidal nets: the case of Tanzania in 2011. Malaria Jour, 12:150
[9] Koenker HM, Yukich JO Mkindi A et al. 2013. Analysing and recommending options for maintaining universal coverage with long-lasting insecticidal nets: the case of Tanzania in 2011. Malaria Jour, 12:150

the health facility. ITNs are also provided on an as-needed basis to households with confirmed malaria cases as part of the malaria case notification strategy.

Progress since PMI was launched

Mainland
Key achievements for the three distribution channels used on the Mainland include:

Universal coverage campaign (UCC): The last universal coverage campaign in 2010-2011 distributed 17.6 million ITNs. A second universal coverage campaign began in mid-2015 and will deliver 22.3 million ITNs, one ITN for every two people, across 22 of the 25 regions on the Mainland. It is scheduled to finish by April 2016. PMI contributed 2.1 million ITNs for this campaign, which will be used to cover the regions for Kigoma and Kagera.

School-based net distribution program: The school net program (SNP) distributes free nets annually to school children in first, third, fifth, seventh, ninth, and eleventh grades. The first round of the SNP was completed in May 2013 and the second in August 2014, both delivering about 500,000 ITNs to all primary and secondary schools in 19 districts in three regions in the south of the country (Ruvuma, Lindi, and Mtwara). An evaluation of the first round showed promising outcomes. The evaluation of the second round is underway and evidence will be used by the United Republic of Tanzania to guide decisions on whether this approach will be continued and scale up to national level.

Tanzania National Voucher Scheme (TNVS)/ Delivery of free ITNs through ANC: The TNVS began in November 2004 with support from the Global Fund to improve the availability of ITNs to pregnant women through ANC clinics. With PMI support beginning in 2006, the program was expanded to include delivery of vouchers to infants at vaccination clinics. The scheme introduced e-vouchers, based on SMS technology, in late 2011 and by 2013 these represented more than half of vouchers redeemed. At its peak in 2013 almost 2 million ITNs were redeemed through the TNVS scheme, approximately half through ANC and half through vaccination clinics. However, in some areas individuals took advantage of inadequate attention to the e-voucher system's security and fraud was discovered. The sole funder of the TNVS at that time, DIFD, withdrew support in June 2014. Months before the end of the TNVS, PMI agreed with NMCP and partners that beginning in 2016 it would support delivery of ITNs to pregnant women at ANC visits and, to the degree possible, through vaccination clinics. Negotiations and planning with the Director Preventive Services, the NMCP, the Prime Minister's Office – Regional Administration and Local Government (PMO-RALG), and other non-government partners, resulted in a call of development of a new approach for direct delivery of ITNs by health workers to pregnant women on their first ANC visit. The details of this system are still being worked out and a project to run this new delivery system will be selected.

Zanzibar
The ZAMEP implemented its first UCC in March of 2012 and distributed 660,000 ITNs. The distribution of ITNs overlapped with the 2011/2012 THMIS survey in Zanzibar. As a result, only a partial effect of the UCC was captured in the THMIS. This may account for results that showed a slight drop in ownership and use from the 2010 DHS and the 2011/2012 THMIS; ownership of at least one ITN dropped from 76% to 74%; usage among children fell from 55% to 51% and among pregnant women from 50% to 36%. Low access is probably a contributor to this relatively low use; however,

results also indicate that in some areas of Zanzibar behavioral issues are a major factor contributing to low use. An example of this is in Kaskazini Pemba District where access (the proportion of the population living with one ITN per two people) was 72% but use was only 41%. In spite of insufficient ITN coverage and low use in some areas, the overall protection in Zanzibar was found to be 95%, as measured by the percentage that slept the previous night under an ITN or in a dwelling sprayed with IRS in the past 12 months (2011/2012 THMIS).

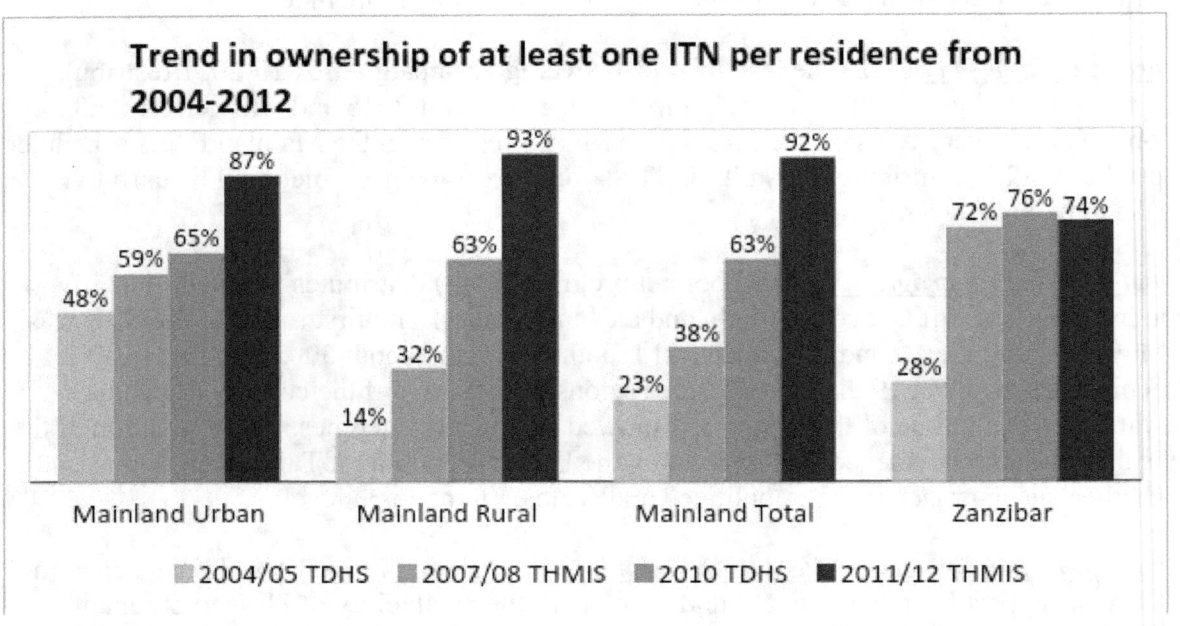

Trend in ownership of at least one ITN per residence from 2004-2012

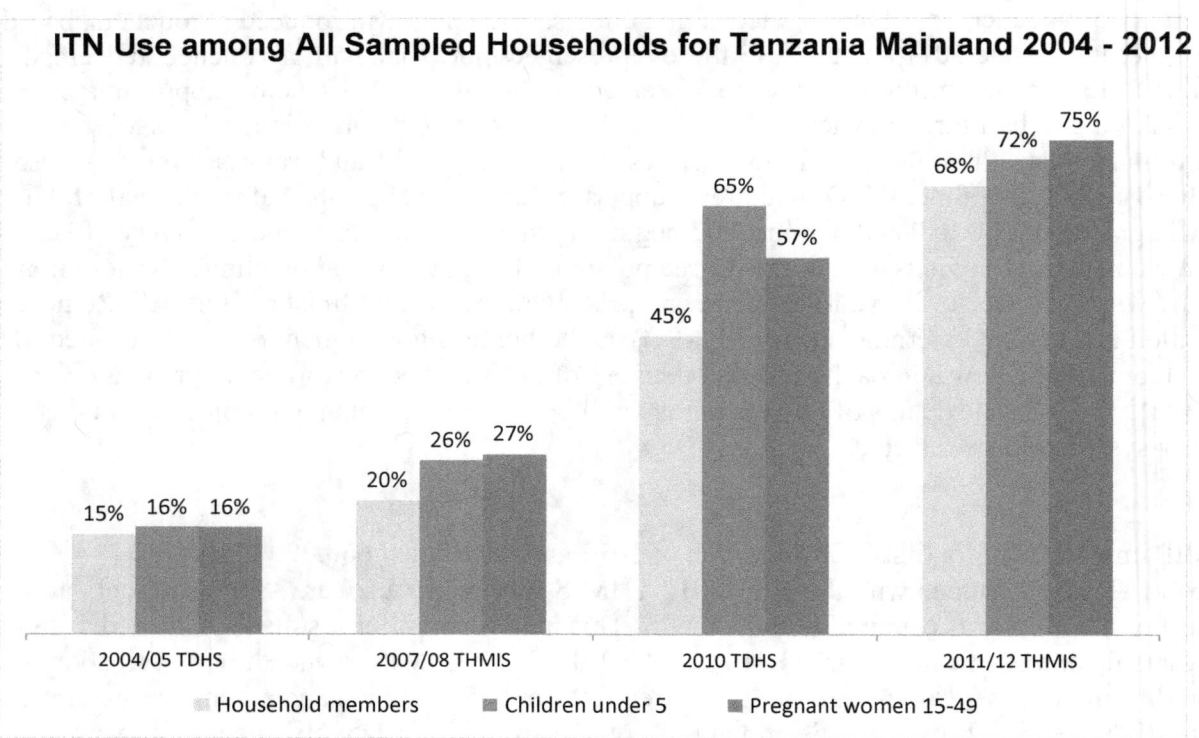

ITN Use among All Sampled Households for Tanzania Mainland 2004 - 2012

28

Progress during the last 12- 18 months

Mainland

In 2014, PMI procured 500,000 ITNs for the school-based net distribution program in Tanzania. In August, the SNP-2 reached 2,337 schools, provided ITNs to 473,700 students, 25,269 teachers and distributed a total 507,775 ITNs in the regions for Ruvuma, Linda, and Mtwara. PMI also procured 2.1 million ITN for the universal coverage campaign that began in June 2015 and will be completed in April 2016. PMI procured ITNs will cover the Kigoma and Kagera Regions.

Zanzibar

In June 2014, Zanzibar launched its ITN continuous distribution strategy. By December, 165,188 ITNs were delivered to health facilities and communities for distribution. Of those, 144,394 have been issued: 22,242 through ANC clinics, 17,861 through vaccination clinics and 65,501 through the community based system.

Commodity gap analysis

Table IIa. ITN Gap Analysis - Mainland

Calendar Year	2015	2016	2017
National Total Targeted Population **PMI Target Population[1]()**	47,255,275 *(12,556,399)*	48,531,167 *(12,895,422)*	49,841,509 *(13,243,598)*
Continuous Distribution Needs[2]			
National Channel #1: ANC **PMI ITNs needs for Mainland()**	1,812,371 *(570,941)*	1,861,305 *(597,980)*	1,911,560 *(626,970)*
National Channel #2:School based[3] **PMI ITNs needs for Mainland()**	500,000 *(500,000)*	1,929,919 *(500,000)*	3,612,794 *(1,034,619)*
Estimated Total Need for Continuous **PMI Estimated Total Need for Mainland ()**	2,312,371 *(1,070,941)*	3,791,224 *(1,097,980)*	5,524,354 *(1,661,589)*
Mass Distribution Needs			
2015/2016 mass distribution campaign	14,400,000	9,848,913	0
Estimated Total Need for Campaign[4]	14,400,000	9,848,913	0

Total Calculated Need: Routine and Campaign	16,712,371	13,640,137	5,524,354
Partner Contributions			
ITNs from Global Fund Round 8 & NFM (mass campaign only)	12,300,000	7,600,000	0[5]
ITNs from PMI funding	2,600,000[6]	1,250,000	1,665,000
Total ITNs Available	**14,900,000**	**8,850,000**	**1,665,000**
Total ITN Surplus (Gap) *PMI Estimated ITN Surplus (Gap)*	**(1,812,371)**[7] *(570,941)*	**(4,790,137)** *152,020[8]*	**(3,859,354)** *3,411[8]*

Footnotes:
1. PMI takes on responsibility for seven of the highest malaria endemic areas on the Mainland (four in the Lake Zone and three in the South).
2. Continuous distribution needs are based on modeling using NetCALC for Year 1 (2016) and Year 2 (2017) following a universal coverage campaign.
3. The quantity of ITNs needed for the school net program in the 22 regions receiving ITNs through the UCC is calculated as the difference between the NetCALC projected need and the ANC delivery target.
4. The three Southern Regions that are covered annually by the school net program were not included in the universal coverage campaign. The total need for the country is calculated as the total population, less the population in those three regions, divided by 1.8 and spread over the two years of the rolling campaign.
5. The Global Fund contributions under the New Funding Mechanism for 2017 are not yet known.
6. PMI contributions for 2015 include 500,000 ITNs for the SNP and 2.1 million ITNs for the universal coverage campaign.
7. In 2015, there was no mechanism for delivery of ITN through ANC clinics. In 2016, a new delivery approach through ANC will be undertaken by PMI and is expected to reach up to seven regions of the country.
8. For PMI target regions there is a surplus of ITNs for continuous distribution. PMI will these surplus ITNs to cover additional high endemic regions through the SNP channel.

Table IIb. ITN Gap Analysis – Zanzibar

Calendar Year	2015	2016	2017
National Total Targeted Population	1,416,163	1,458,648	1,502,407
Continuous Distribution Needs			
Zanzibar Channel #1: ANC	63,727	65,512	68,460
Zanzibar Channel #2:EPI delivery	56,646	58,322	60,853
Zanzibar channel #3: Community-based	112,814	118,139	121,445
Zanzibar Channel #4: Reactive Case Detection	1,000	1,000	1,000
Estimated Total Need for Continuous[1]	234,187	242,973[2]	251,758[2]
Mass Distribution Needs			
2016 mass distribution campaign	0	810,360	0
Estimated Total Need for Campaigns	0	810,360	0
Total Calculated Need: Routine and Campaign	**234,187**	**1,053,333**	**251,758**
Partner Contributions			
ITNs carried over from previous year	0	0	0
ITNs from Global Fund Round 8 & NFM	234,187	670,000[3]	0
ITNs planned with PMI funding	0	238,000[4]	251,758[4]
Total ITNs Available	**234,187**	**908,000**	**251,758**
Total ITN Surplus (Gap)	**0**	**(145,333)**	**0**

Footnotes:
1. Estimated needs for continuous are based on NetCalc models and assume no Universal Coverage Campaign.
2. If there is a Universal Coverage Campaign in 2015 or 2016, the need for ITNs through continuous distribution channels will be adjusted to reflect the lower needs.
3. These ITNs are under review as part of the pending Zanzibar Global Fund Concept Note.
4. PMI funded ITNs will be used to support continuous distribution. If there is a universal coverage campaign, PMI will reprogram funds to address the lowered needs for continuous distribution in the first two years following a campaign.

31

Plans and justification

Mainland
The distribution of 22 million ITNs across 22 of the 25 Regions of Mainland Tanzania will be completed by mid-2016. The Tanzania National Malaria Strategic Plan: 2014-2020 calls for continuous distribution to maintain high coverage, which includes delivery of nets to pregnant women at ANC clinics, infants at vaccination clinics, and school children through the SNP. The MoHSW, PMO-RALG, and development partners established the broad outlines of a system to delivery ITNs, free of charge, to women at ANC clinics. This may be expanded to deliver ITNs through vaccination clinics depending on adequate resources. PMI will be the principal donor for this new system which is due to begin in high malaria endemic areas in the Lake Zone (Mwanza, Geita, Kagera, and Mara Regions) and the South (Mtwara, Lindi and Ruvuma Regions) in early 2016.

PMI will also expand its support for the SNP to reach those same seven regions. In 2017, nets delivered in the campaign will be between one and two years old. The number of ITNs needed to maintain high ITN coverage across the population in the first two years following a universal coverage campaign is less that required in later years . Adjusting earlier projected needs[10] to the target population in the seven regions covered by PMI, indicates that about 1 million ITNs will be needed in the first year and 1.5 million in the second year following a universal coverage campaign to maintain high coverage. The three southern regions, not being part of the campaign, will continue to receive at least 500,000 ITNs annually through the SNP.

Zanzibar
In 2012 Zanzibar completed a universal coverage campaign, delivering over 660,000 ITNs, and has requested Global Fund support for a universal coverage campaign in 2016. The PMI FY 2016 planning assumes that there would be no universal coverage campaign. If ITNs for a UCC in 2016 are provided, PMI will need to adjust this FY 2016 proposal. The FY 2016 funding level is based on models to determine the needed inputs of ITN to maintain high coverage.

Proposed activities with FY 2016 funding:($13,585,200)

Mainland
1. *Procure 1.665 million ITNs:* PMI will procure about 1 million ITNs for the SNP and about 665,000 for delivery through ANC clinics. *($5,500,000)*
2. *Distribution costs for ITNs through ANC Clinics and to primary schools through the School Net Program and technical assistance for NMCP and ZAMEP. ($7,710,000)*
   a. *ITN Distribution:* Transportation of 1.6 million ITNs from port of entry to all health facilities (for ANC) and to schools (for SNP) in 7 PMI-focus regions (estimated cost $1.2/ITN; total of $2m)
   b. *Provide ITN-related supply chain technical assistance:* Strengthen the quality of the ITN supply chain delivery system through specific activities, including: conducting audits to

---

[10] Koenker HM, Yukich JO Mkindi A et al. 2013. Analysing and recommending options for maintaining universal coverage with long-lasting insecticidal nets: the case of Tanzania in 2011. Malaria Jour, 12:150

detect/prevent leakages, improved quantification practices, supportive supervision, etc. (estimated costs $1.25/ITN; total of $2.1m)

    c. *Strengthen the capacity of facility-based ITN distribution:* provide technical assistance and support to ensure that ITN distribution activities in health care facilities are successfully designed, introduced and incorporated into the comprehensive ANC clinic services. Specific support may include: (estimated costs $1.25/ITN; total of $2.1m)

        i. one-time start up costs (initial training, ANC register revisions, production of revised job aids)

        ii. annual recurring operational costs (supportive supervision etc)

    d. *Technical assistance to NMCP and ZAMEP for vector control* (estimated costs $800.000)

3. *BCC to increase demand, improve use, and foster improved care of ITNs:* Targeted messaging will be used to increase uptake of ITN through ANC and schools and to improve use and care of ITNs. *(See BCC section for details)*

Zanzibar

1. *Procure 251,758 ITNs for Zanzibar continuous distribution*: ITNs for continuous distribution to pregnant women through ANC clinics, to infants through vaccination clinics, and through community-based approaches. *($830,000)*

2. *Support for distribution of ITNs through continuous channels*: PMI will support distribution of ITNs though health facility routine services and through a community-based approach *($185,200)*

3. *BCC to increase demand, improve use, and foster improved care of ITNs:* Targeted messaging will be used to increase uptake of ITN through ANC, vaccination clinics and community based system, and to improve use and care of ITNs. *(See BCC section for details)*

2. Indoor residual spraying

NMCP/ZAMEP/PMI objectives

Mainland

The NMCP Strategic Plan 2014-2020 calls for application of quality IRS in selected areas and maintenance of coverage at near the current level of 14% in Mainland Tanzania. To maintain optimal protection with ITNs, the NMCP recommends that pyrethroid insecticides not be used for IRS.

Zanzibar

The Zanzibar malaria elimination goal is to achieve 100% coverage with IRS or ITNs by 2015 by achieving 95% coverage of IRS in the target areas, and 90% ITN use in non-IRS areas. The ZAMEP strategy follows the PMI adopted approach of moving from blanket spraying, which was done in all ten districts in Zanzibar, to targeted spraying in districts showing high malaria transmission, then shifting to focal spraying once malaria transmission is highly localized and sound surveillance can identify those hot spots *(shehias* reporting at least 4 or more weekly cases and a 1.5 fold increase in weekly cases compared to the average from previous three weeks). Zanzibar has also adopted a strategy of focal spraying of hot spots both proactively based on previous evidence of persistent transmission in an area and reactive to outbreaks.

Mainland and Zanzibar

IRS activities in Tanzania ensure protection of the environment and safe disposal of waste in accordance with the approved Pesticide Evaluation Report and Safe Use Action Plans. Environmental inspection visits are conducted regularly to assess compliance with US Government and Tanzanian national environmental standards.

Progress since PMI was launched

Mainland

Since 2007, the NCMP has focused spraying in 18 districts in Lake Zone. The 2010 DHS shows that the Lake Zone had the highest under-five mortality rate of 109/1,000 live births, above the national average of 81/1,000 live births. Malaria prevalence among children 6-59 months of age in the Lake Zone, at 34%, was also the highest in Tanzania (2007/2008 THMIS).

After several rounds of blanket (entire region sprayed) and targeted (entire districts, but not all districts in a regions) IRS, combined with high ITN coverage following mass universal coverage campaigns between 2009-2011, the prevalence in the Lake Zone fell from 34% to 14% (2011/2012 THMIS). The region with the greatest reduction in the Lake Zone was Kagera, where prevalence fell from 41% (2007/2008 THMIS) to 8% (2011/2012 THMIS). With this and other data indicating success after blanket spraying multiple times, PMI and the NMCP moved from blanket to targeted spraying in the Lake Zone.

With increasing evidence of resistance following spray rounds in 2010/2011, the strategy in the Lake Zone changed and a carbamate insecticide (bendiocarb) was used in 2011/2012 in two districts. This was expanded to all 18 districts in 2012/2013. The strategy was then changed again in 2013 following further evidence of resistance and in 2013, and in 2014 and 2015 pirimiphos-methyl CS was introduced.

Zanzibar

After six rounds of blanket spraying (2006-2011), Zanzibar moved to a combination of target and focal spraying for two years (2012-2013). For each round, household coverage was over 90%. Based on the low malaria prevalence, combined with a robust and reliable surveillance and entomological monitoring systems, in 2014 and 2015 Zanzibar shifted from target and focal spraying focal spraying only, and using malaria incidence as the criteria for selection of villages (*shehia*).

IRS Scale-down phases and timing in Zanzibar

Spray phase	2006 - 2007	2007- 2008	2008- 2009	2009- 2010	2010- 2011	2011- 2012	2012- 2013	2013- 2014	2014- 2015
Blanket (Knock-down)									
Targeted (Keep-down)									
Focal (Keep-low)									

– **Blanket** to knock-down transmission (or knock-down further) in entire regions
– **Targeted** to maintain low transmission in particular districts with high/increasing transmission
– **Focal** to address specific "hot spots" where higher transmission persists

Table IIIa: PMI-supported IRS activities in Mainland Tanzania: 2012-2017

Year	No. Districts Sprayed	Insecticide Used	No. Structures Sprayed	Coverage Rate	Population Protected
2011/2012	18 (targeted)	Pyrethroid (P) 16 districts Carbamate (C) 2 districts	1,224,095	93%	6,518,120
2012/2013	18 (targeted)	Pyrethroid (P) 11 districts Carbamate (C) 18 districts	659,146 (P and C areas) 114,783 (re-spray C areas)	95%	3,496,421 (P and C areas) 555,932 (re-spray C areas)
2014	15 (targeted)	Carbamate (C) 9 districts Pirimiphos-Methyl CS (OP) 6 districts	108,173 (re-spray remaining C areas) 385,252 (OP areas)	90% 92%	555,503 (C areas) 1,918,180 (OP areas)
2015	7 (targeted)	Pirimiphos-Methyl CS (OP)	389,714	93%	1,930,230
2016	7 (targeted)	Pirimiphos-Methyl CS (OP)	418,000	~90%	~2,000,000
2017	7 (targeted)	Carbamate (C)	350,000	~90%	~1,500,000

Table IIIb: PMI-supported IRS activities on Zanzibar: 2012-2017

Year	No. Districts Sprayed	Insecticide Used	No. Structures Sprayed	Coverage Rate	Population Protected
2012	9 (targeted)	Carbamate (C)	141,858	95%	586,657
2013	9 (targeted)	Carbamate (C)	51,904	96%	250,505
2014	8 (focal)	Carbamate (C) Pirimiphos-Methyl CS (OP)	4,250 (re-spray in select C areas) 62,076 (OP areas)	95%	312,340
2015	8 (focal)	Pirimiphos-Methyl CS (OP)	66,497	95%	339,135
2016	8 (focal)	Pirimiphos-Methyl CS (OP)	25,000	~90%	~125,000
2017	8 (focal)	Carbamate (C)	20,000	~90%	~100,000

Progress during the last 12- 18 months

Mainland

In 2015, the Mainland maintained the Lake Zone's 2014 spray target of about 450,000 structures, protecting just under 2 million people. PMI continued its contribution to a public-private partnership by supplying insecticide to Geita Gold Mine, which contributed approximately $200,000 towards the operational costs of the spraying in the area of Geita Town Council.

Results from entomological monitoring, insecticide resistance monitoring and residual insecticidal activity following IRS on the Tanzania Mainland are presented in the Monitoring and Evaluation section.

Zanzibar

In 2015, Zanzibar continued the focal spraying that was implemented in 2014. In 2015 all villages (*shehias*) that showed malaria incidence of more than 7 cases/1,000 population were sprayed. Just over 66,000 structures were sprayed, protecting 330,000 people. This was consistent with the numbers reached in 2014.

Plans and justification

The IRS in 2016 will be the third consecutive year of spraying with pirimiphos-methyl. In consultation with the NMCP, the ZAMEP, and key partners, the decision was made to move from pirimiphos-methyl to another non-pyrethroid insecticide in 2017, which may require two rounds of spraying. This proposed preemptive rotation is in agreement with PMI guidelines that suggest this approach may be the best way to prolong susceptibility and maximize the long-term cost effectiveness of insecticides. A final decision on this proposed rotation will be made based on the most recent resistance data.

Mainland

The NMCP is committed to achieving and maintaining universal ITN coverage and has launched a second ITN universal coverage campaign to be completed by mid-2016. PMI has funded IRS in Tanzania for nine years, but with limited resources it is not possible to support large scale use of both approaches. Thus the role of IRS in Tanzania has been evolving in recent years from that of a major control intervention to an intervention with more targeted applications. The role of IRS is now seen as a tool to mitigate mosquito resistance to pyrethoids and to supplement ITNs in areas of persistent, high malaria transmission in the Lake Zone.

The principal criteria used to determine which areas to spray in the Lake Zone include: 1) overall malaria positivity rates and 2) incidence, as determined using health facility reports and recent census data. Operational factors are also considered. While this approach has limitations, including poor quality of data, lack of true representativeness of the population, and using past reporting periods for current decision-making, at present these are the best available criteria for selecting IRS areas.

Zanzibar

In 2012, Zanzibar achieved universal coverage with ITNs and thus began to scale-down IRS. Zanzibar also has a strong entomological and epidemiologic surveillance system that provides real-time data for epidemic detection and response. The ZAMEP will spray known hot spots from the previous year.

Proposed activities with FY 2016 funding: ($9,250,000)

Mainland
1. _Procure insecticide and support spraying in the Lake Zone._ PMI will support targeted IRS in the Lake Zone reaching approximately 350,000 structures and protecting about 1.5 million persons. PMI also proposes a switch from a pirimiphos-methyl formulation that will have been used for the three previous years to another non-pyrethroid insecticide in 2017. PMI will also continue to support the public-private partnership with Geita Gold Mine. _($8,750,000)_
2. _BCC to maintain high acceptance of IRS. (See BCC section for details)_

Zanzibar
1. _Focal spraying._ PMI will support focal spraying in hot spots, covering about 20,000 structures and protecting 100,000 people. _($500,000)_
2. _BCC to maintain high acceptance of IRS. (See BCC section for details)_

3. Malaria in pregnancy

NMCP/ZAMEP/PMI objectives

Tanzania implements the three-pronged approach to prevent the adverse effects associated with malaria in pregnancy recommended by the WHO: 1) ITNs through antenatal care clinics, 2) intermittent preventive treatment (IPTp) with sulfadoxine-pyrimethamine (SP), and 3) prompt case management of pregnant women with malaria. The objectives are to achieve 80% coverage of two doses of IPTp, 85% use of ITNs by pregnant women, and 100% prompt case management of malaria infections in pregnancy.

ITNs

Until mid-2014, the TNVS provided e-coupons to women at ANC visits that were redeemable at nearby retail outlets on the Mainland. Zanzibar has implemented a continuous long-lasting ITN distribution strategy which includes free provision of a net to pregnant women at their first ANC visit.

IPTp

Mainland

The MoHSW has adopted the updated WHO policy of IPTp3+, which is to give three or more doses of SP monthly until the day of delivery, administered as directly observed therapy during ANC visits. In addition, MoHSW has instated a policy of screening women by RDT at their first ANC visit and treating those who test positive according to national guidelines.

Zanzibar

Given the low prevalence of malaria in women at time of delivery (0.8%), Zanzibar no longer implements IPTp and has adopted a policy of screening pregnant women by RDT at the first ANC visit and treating those testing positive according to national guidelines.

Iron/folate

A three-year supply of iron/folate (ferrous sulphate 200mg + folic acid 0.25mg) was purchased with USAID and DFID funds for use in 2014-2016. This combination is provided at ANC according to national policy for prevention and treatment of anemia. High-dose folic acid is procured and provided for pediatric indications only and is not provided at ANC.

Case management of acute malaria

Case management of uncomplicated malaria in pregnancy follows WHO recommendations. For severe malaria in the first trimester, parenteral quinine remains the nationally recommended treatment pending further evidence of injectable artesunate safety, while treatment in the second and third trimesters is parenteral artesunate.

Progress since PMI was launched

The TNVS, which provided highly subsidized ITNs to pregnant women on the Mainland, was introduced in 2004 as part of a keep-up strategy between universal campaigns. The TNVS achieved its goal of distributing 2 million nets in 2013 but was defunded in 2014 after reports of provider fraud. Net use among pregnant women was at 76% on the Mainland in 2012 but at only 36% in Zanzibar (THMIS) after universal coverage campaigns in 2011-2012. Zanzibar implemented continuous distribution in

2014 via ANC as part of a strategy that also includes routine net distribution at EPI visits, reactive case detection visits, and community-based distribution as needed.

Since 2006, PMI and maternal health funding has focused on rolling out the national training on focused antenatal care (FANC), a package of antenatal services which includes IPTp. Cumulatively, 7,181 providers from 3,540 facilities have been trained, covering 74% and 100% of FANC facilities on the Mainland and Zanzibar, respectively. PMI has also supported development of a pre-service malaria in pregnancy training curriculum, which has contributed to approximately 1,600 new graduates with FANC skills each year since 2006. Training in antenatal care continues when District Health Management Teams invest their own budgets and use PMI-trained trainers to conduct further training within their district.

ANC attendance is almost universal (94% of pregnant women make at least two visits; 2010 DHS), yet IPTp2 uptake has remained at approximately 30% (see table below). The Malaria in Pregnancy Task Force, a group composed of members from the NMCP, the Reproductive and Child Health group and other relevant stakeholders, has been working to address challenges in SP availability and IPTp uptake, and recently supported the adoption and rollout of IPTp3+ policy. The Ministry-led Safe Motherhood Campaign (*Wazazi Nipendeni*), launched in 2012, has been spreading IPTp messages through multimedia campaigns.

IPTp uptake in Tanzania

Intervention	2004/05 DHS	2007 THMIS	2009/10 DHS	2012 THMIS
Percentage of women who took at least one dose of SP at ANC during their last pregnancy (IPTp 1)	53%	57%	60%	60%
Percentage of women who took at least two doses of SP at ANC during their last pregnancy (IPTp 2)	22%	30%	26%	33%

Progress during the last 12- 18 months

Currently there is no mechanism for distribution of ITNs via ANC on the Mainland. After the TNVS was stopped in 2014, PMI supported a scoping exercise to identify new approaches for routine distribution. Based on this exercise, the MoHSW, PMO-RALG, and development partners have established the broad outlines of a system to delivery ITNs, free of charge, to women at ANC clinics. PMI will be the principal donor for this new system which is due to begin in high malaria endemic areas in the Lake Zone (Regions of Mwanza, Geita, Kagera, and Mara) and the South (Regions of Mtwara, Lindi, and Ruvuma) in early 2016. Further details can be found in the ITN section of the MOP. In the meantime, a universal coverage campaign delivering 22.3 million nets to 22 of 25 regions on the Mainland will begin in mid-2015. In June 2014, Zanzibar launched its ITN continuous distribution strategy and has delivered 22,242 ITNs through ANC clinics as of April 2015.

With support from the MIP Task Force, the NMCP updated the IPTp policy (IPTp3+) in all national documents including FANC guidelines, the National Guidelines for Malaria Diagnosis and Treatment, and the 2014 version of the HMIS Reproductive and Child Health book. The IPTp3+ policy was officially adopted by the MoHSW in 2014 and PMI supported the training of 338 staff at public dispensaries during Phase II of the rollout in 2014-2015 (staff at public hospitals and health centers were trained in advance of policy adoption). HMIS registers have also been updated to record up to four doses of IPTp.

In 2015, PMI partners are conducting pre-service MIP education at 20 health training institutions and quality improvement through training and supervision of over 400 health facility staff across 88 districts in Kagera and Mara Regions on FANC, including MIP and the updated IPTp3+ policy. The Linking Initiatives For Elimination of pediatric HIV (LIFE) program is leveraging existing PMTCT and MNCH platforms to train staff and improve quality of MIP services in all 13 district CHMTs and all PMTCT/RCH clinics in Lindi (213 clinics) and Mtwara (190 clinics). Both projects are also performing quarterly tracking of SP stocks at health facilities and conducting feedback meetings with regional and District Health Management Teams to improve SP availability.

PMI also supported the completion and evaluation of Phase I of the Safe Motherhood Campaign, which was designed to improve uptake of all ANC services, including IPTp and nets, through a multimedia campaign. Phase II of the campaign, emphasizing IPTp3+, will be launched in mid-2015 and will build on lessons learned from the first phase, including a focus on potential complications caused by MIP, which were not well known by women. Phase II will utilize channels at the community and local level where underserved women will be reached (rather than relying on mass media), refine the SMS campaign to reach a greater proportion of women, and link messaging campaigns with service providers so that they are aware of the content of the interventions and can reiterate/complement the messages during visits.

Commodity gap analysis

SP is procured by the Tanzanian government; thus, PMI has no plans to procure SP. However, there have been persistent challenges in getting this stock to the peripheral facilities. PMI is working to address this problem to ensure availability at facilities with ANC clinics.

Table IV. SP Gap Analysis for Malaria in Pregnancy

Calendar Year	2015	2016	2017
Total Population*	47,255,481	48,531,379	49,841,726
SP Needs			
Total number of pregnant women attending ANC **	1,852,415	1,902,430	1,953,796
Number of ANC visits per woman	3	3	3
Total number of IPTp treatments***	3,334,347	3,424,374	3,516,832
Maintenance of 9-15 MOS stock at MSD	693,556	2,782,378	2,846,619
Total SP Need (in treatments)	**4,027,903**	**6,206,752**	**6,363,451**
Partner Contributions			
SP carried over (deficit) from previous year	0	0	0
SP from MOH	2,463,333	6,206,752	6,363,451
SP from Global Fund	0	0	0
SP from Other Donors	0	0	0
SP planned with PMI funding	0	0	0
Total SP Available	**2,463,333**	**6,206,752**	**6,363,451**
Total SP Surplus (Gap)	**(1,564,570)**	**-**	**-**

*Total population obtained from 2012 National Census plus a growth rate of 2.7% per year.
**Calculated assuming that 4% of the population is pregnant and 96% of pregnant women attend ANC
***Calculated assuming that % of pregnant women receiving IPTp1 = 80%, IPTp2 = 60%, IPTp3 = 40%

Plans and justification

Following on the successful rollout of and training on the new IPTp guidelines in 2014-2016, PMI will support continued training and supervision for IPTp3+ and case management integrated with family planning, maternal and child health, and HIV programming. Because IPTp2 uptake has not increased even in the 251 health facilities that PMI partners have been working in over the past few years (48% in 2012, 47% in 2013, and dropping to 29% in 2014, partially because the project ended early in the year), FY 2016 funding will continue activities initiated with FY 2015 funds that attain greater geographic coverage of high burden areas. In addition, results-based financing (see HSS section for more information) with IPTp2+ and SP availability as indicators will be initiated, and will provide cash incentives to individual health care providers as well as health facilities. BCC to boost ITN use, ANC attendance, and IPTp uptake will continue. PMI will support provision of long-lasting ITNs to pregnant women through continuous distribution at ANC on the Mainland and Zanzibar.

Proposed activities with FY 2016 funding: ($1,000,000)

PMI's funding for the following activities will contribute to a larger effort funded by other USAID health programs to improve demand for and the quality of antenatal care on the Mainland, including malaria prevention and treatment of acute infections.

Mainland

1. _Refresher trainings and integrated supportive supervision for MIP interventions in 8 regions._ Health facility-based activities will expand from four regions in the Lake and Southern Zones to an additional four high-burden regions with FY 2016 funds. PMI will support training, quality improvement, and supervision of IPTp3+and malaria case management within the integrated ANC platform. _($1,000,000)_
2. _ITN keep-up program at ANC._ PMI will support the procurement and distribution of ITNs for continuous distribution to pregnant women at their first ANC visit (_Included in ITN budget_)
3. _BCC activities to promote IPTp3+ and ITNs._ Efforts initiated by the Safe Motherhood Campaign will continue through co-investments supported by HIV, family planning, and MCH funds to ensure that ANC clients are counseled on the importance of ANC attendance, IPTp3+, and ITN use. BCC materials will be printed and disseminated systematically, targeting regions where malaria prevalence is high and IPTp uptake is low. This activity includes leaflets and other promotional materials in health facilities as well as media messages in the community. _(Included in BCC budget)_
4. _Supply chain support._ PMI is working to address the problem of SP stockouts at ANC facilities through a national commodities electronic tracking and requisition system to ensure more consistent supplies of the drug, sulfadoxine-pyrimethamine, for IPTp at ANC clinics. PMI will support strengthening of quantification for malaria commodities, transportation, storage, inventory management, and end-use verification. _(Included in Case Management budget)_

Zanzibar

1. _Refresher Supportive supervision at ANC._ PMI will support regular antenatal clinic supervisory visits by ministry staff, which will cover supervision of the test and treat policy and prevention and case management activities. _(Included in integrated supportive supervision budget)_
2. _ITN keep-up program at ANC._ PMI will support the procurement and distribution of ITNs for continuous distribution to pregnant women at their first ANC visit (_Included in ITN budget_)
3. _BCC activities to promote ITNs._ Mass media messaging and printed materials will be dispersed to promote early uptake of ITNs at ANC visits. Community mobilization via _shehia_ health custodian committees will also be included. _(Included in BCC budget)_

4. Case management

a. Diagnosis and Treatment

NMCP/ZAMEP/PMI objectives

The goal of the NMCP strategy is to achieve universal access to high quality malaria diagnostic testing and treatment in both public and private health facilities. The national targets for the 2014-2020 National Malaria Medium-Term Strategic Plan for case management are to increase to 80% the proportion of children under five years of age who: 1) receive appropriate diagnosis and treatment within 24 hours of onset of fever, and 2) receive appropriate management of both uncomplicated and severe malaria according to national treatment guidelines. The NMCP's continuing priorities for 2017 are: to improve the quality of diagnostic and case management services; to maintain and improve antimalarial drug supplies in the public sector; to improve access, quality, and affordable ACTs in the private sector; to strengthen the pharmacovigilance system; and to strengthen therapeutic drug efficacy monitoring.

As on the Mainland, the Zanzibar malaria strategy calls for parasitological confirmation for all patients with fever. Through PMI support, ZAMEP has been able to enhance microscopy at hospitals and larger facilities and to provide mRDT testing training to all government and some private health facilities. This has enabled the program to meet its objective of operating the well-functioning Malaria Early Epidemic Detection System (MEEDS; see Monitoring and Evaluation section for more information).

Both the NMCP and ZAMEP diagnostic and treatment guidelines call for referral of patients with severe malaria from lower level facilities to the nearest health center after first giving the patient an intramuscular injection of artesunate. Intramuscular artemether or quinine can be used as second-line drugs if artesunate is not available. Use of rectal artesunate is also permitted if injection is not feasible.

Progress since PMI was launched

Mainland
ACTs were officially launched in Mainland Tanzania on December 15, 2006. The NMCP adopted artemether-lumefantrine (AL) as the first-line drug with artesunate-amodiaquine (ASAQ) as an alternative, second line drug for the treatment of uncomplicated malaria. Recently dihydroartemisin-piperaquin (DP) has also been recommended as an alternative ACT. In 2013 the NMCP revised the national treatment guidelines to include injectable artesunate for the treatment of severe malaria. PMI has supported several interventions to improve access to ACTs and case management at the health facility level. Through the three Zonal Resource Centers of Arusha, Iringa, and Kigoma PMI supported the training of 3,955 health workers in comprehensive malaria case management, including management of severe malaria and malaria in pregnancy. PMI also supported the NMCP to do nationwide training of healthcare workers on the new treatment guidelines: 819 public health centers and hospitals have been covered and the NMCP has now begun implementation at the dispensary level.

Since 2006, PMI has supported the procurement and scale-up of RDTs, assisted the MoHSW's Diagnostic Services Section to conduct comprehensive malaria diagnostics training sessions at the National Health Laboratory and Quality Assurance Training Center (NHLQATC), and worked with partners to develop a Malaria Reference Laboratory within the NHLQATC. PMI supported therapeutic efficacy monitoring conducted at eight sentinel sites in 2011 and 2012 to assess in vivo efficacy of ACT. The monitoring was hampered by enrollment that was both slower and lower than expected and by the fact that many of the cases had an insufficient number of parasites. Nevertheless the results clearly showed that the efficacy at 28 days of two ACT combinations studied, AL and ASAQ, was over 95%.

NMCP guidelines state that all suspected malaria cases should be confirmed by a recommended malaria test prior to treatment. Microscopic examination of Giemsa-strained blood films remains a cornerstone of malaria diagnosis throughout Tanzania, but is only available at regional and district hospitals and some health centers (about 20% of all health facilities) therefore most health facilities use RDTs to confirm malaria cases. With PMI and Global Fund support the NMCP completed implementation of RDT provision to all government health facilities in all districts in November 2012. During the RDT rollout a total of 9,647 routine RDT testers were trained (2 from each health facility) out of a total of 11,765 trained health service providers as part of a program of cascade training in health facilities. Between 14 and 16 million RDT are procured yearly. Malaria RDT quantification is based on the assumption that all cases of fever will be tested for malaria parasites: 90% by RDTs and 10% by microscopy. Lot testing of RDT kits is coordinated by the NMCP using a WHO protocol and random samples sent to Institut Pasteur du Cambodge in Cambodia. The Medical Stores Department (MSD), Tanzania's central medical store, sends random samples of RDT kits to Ifakara Health Institute as part of their internal quality checks of stored products before shipment to the MSD zonal stores. Previous assessments have shown that the quality of both malaria microscopy and RDT testing is very poor at almost all levels of the health system. [11]

The NMCP intends to improve the quality of malaria diagnosis via the continuance of RDT and microscopy training and the establishment of a functional QA/QC system within the existing healthcare system infrastructure. PMI has extensively supported NMCP in this goal. From November 2009 through August 2013 PMI partners supported the NMCP to conduct 10 two-week training sessions that certified 160 laboratory workers from all regions to be expert malaria microscopists. These personnel serve as resource malaria microscopists at regional and district hospitals and some health centers. This exceeded the target of one person certified from each of the 133 districts. In addition, PMI supported the evaluation and quality assurance project conducted in 2012 in 16 hospital laboratories (microscopy) and 48 representative health facilities (RDT) in both the Mainland and Zanzibar. This evaluation showed that RDT testing accuracy at baseline was poor to extremely poor. Deficiencies noted included: incorrect sample and buffer volumes, incorrect incubation times, and improper identification of invalid test results. These findings were primarily attributed to an absence of effective program RDT testing policies and ineffective training rather than a lack of motivation among HCW. This project was used as the basis for the NMCP's current QA/QC program. PMI also allocated money to establish a National Malaria Slide Bank to be located at the National Health Laboratory. The protocol for the slide bank was approved and sample collection begun in late 2014. As part of the plan for the slide bank the NMCP has also worked with partners to develop a microscopy QA system that will include monthly blinded cross-checking of blood slides by a District supervisor and periodic external QA via blinded positive and

---

[11]WHO: Informal Consultation on Quality Control of Malaria Microscopy , 2006; Reyburn, H., et al; The contribution of microscopy to targeting antimalarial treatment in a low transmission area of Tanzania . 2006; McMorrow ML, et al. Challenges in Routine Implementation and Quality Control of Rapid Diagnostic Tests for Malaria–Rufiji District, Tanzania. 2008

negative samples sent from the slide bank. This proposed system has not yet been fully initiated as it awaits completion of the slide bank. In 2016 the NMCP intends to use Global Fund support to continue microscopy training and QA/QC implementation and to support the NHLQATC to maintain the National Malaria Slide Bank once it is established.

NMCP, with technical support from partners, completed a pilot implementation of RDT testing accuracy QA/QC in Kagera and Pwani Districts. PMI has contracted MalariaCare to work with the NMCP to continue the implementation of this RDT testing accuracy QA system throughout the rest of the Mainland over the next year.

NMCP is working with both the public and private sector to promote universal access to RDTs and ACTs. Current implementation strategies emphasize consolidating universal access to malaria diagnostics in both public and private health facilities, scale-up of diagnostics quality assurance, provision of appropriate management of uncomplicated malaria, and the use of injectable artesunate for treatment of severe malaria. Through the support of the Global Fund and first-line buyers, the availability of quality, affordable ACT will be facilitated in the private sector via a co-pay mechanism. NMCP's anticipated implementation strategies include expansion of RDT diagnostic services to Accredited Drug Dispensing Outlet (ADDOs). There are nearly 4,000 ADDOs and another 2,000 outlets awaiting accreditation by the government. The majority are located in rural areas where access to malaria commodities and testing services is limited.

Improving integrated Community Case Management (iCCM) is a goal of the MoHSW and the major focus is on childhood illnesses including malaria, diarrhea, and pneumonia. The NMCP participated in the development of the National Community Based Health Program Policy (CBHPP) Guidelines to further expand health service activities using Village/Community Health Workers (VHW/CHW) with improved linkages to nearby public health facilities.

Zanzibar

ACTs were deployed for the first time in Zanzibar in 2003 and the current first-line treatment for uncomplicated malaria is ASAQ. The second-line treatment is AL. Injectable artesunate is the drug of choice for severe malaria with quinine or artemether as acceptable alternatives in situations where artesunate is not available. ACTs are widely available in health facilities. The current Zanzibar Malaria Diagnosis & Treatment Guidelines were updated in April 2014 to incorporate various WHO recommendations such as the use of injectable artesunate for treatment of severe malaria, recommended antimalarials for HIV/AIDS patients, and to include the WHO recommendation of the use of single low-dose (0.25 mg base/kg) primaquine for all patients with confirmed uncomplicated *P. falciparum* infection in areas pursuing elimination. PMI provided support to ZAMEP to disseminate the updated guidelines and conduct refresher trainings.

Malaria microscopy QA/QC was established in 2005 at 23 public health facilities in Zanzibar and as of 2015 had been expanded to 77 (51 public, 8 private, 4 faith-based organizations, 14 military). In conjunction with partners, ZAMEP developed a standardized RDT QA/QC system and is planning to develop a similar system for microscopy QA/QC.

Mainland

As noted above, the NMCP and PMI partners completed a pilot implementation of RDT testing accuracy QA/QC in Kagera and Pwani Regions. This QA/QC system relies upon trained personnel from district and regional health management teams to conduct supportive supervision at quarterly intervals targeting at least two healthcare workers in each public health facility that performs RDT testing. This system focuses on five key quality indices: 1) correct blood volume, 2) correct buffer volume, 3) correct reading time, 4) recognizing invalid test results, and 5) correct labeling of the RDT device. With the aid of PMI through an implementing partner, the NMCP is currently rolling out the model to the remaining regions within the Lake Zone with eventual implementation in all regions of the Mainland estimated to be completed by October 2015.

The protocol for the National Slide Bank was approved in 2014. Collection of samples is underway with a first phase target of 80 sets of 240 blood slides each. There will be a total of 4 planned field visits to collect 20 sets per visit. To date one visit has been completed and 20 sets are in place. The second phase of the slide bank project will expand the total number of sets to 160 enabling scale-up and maintenance of the external QA activities. NMCP is working with partners to develop the reporting database program and the NHL through the slide bank program will support training courses on blood film preparation and diagnosis to lab technicians at the regional level with eventual implementation down to the district level.

In the past year the NMCP with PMI support has completed dissemination of the National Diagnostic and Treatment Guidelines to 819 public hospitals and health centers and began dissemination to public dispensaries. The training objectives are 1) to reinforce appropriate practices for care of malaria patients and management of commodities, 2) to instruct healthcare workers on the use of injectable artesunate for the treatment of severe malaria, 3) to orient healthcare workers about the increased IPTp dosing schedule and 4) to introduce the use of RDT and dispensing registers. As of April 2015 dissemination has completed in 169 dispensaries in 17 regions with the remaining eight regions to be completed by July 2015. PMI funds are being used to support Zonal Training Centers to sensitize regional and council management teams about the guidelines and to train additional staff in all public health centers and dispensaries.

PMI has supported, since its inception, the Tibu Homa Project of integrated service delivery in the Lake Zone aimed at improving child health through strengthening the capacity of facility-based health workers to provide fundamental diagnostic and treatment services for malaria and other major causes of severe febrile illness and death in children under five years of age. The project will close in December 2015 and has begun the dissemination of the results. These show that the proportion of children under five years old tested via RDT/microscopy before antimalarial treatment improved, as did the proportion with positive results who received correct antimalarial treatment from a skilled health care worker in the first 24 hours after onset of fever. Supply chain management in the Tibu Homa supported facilities also improved.

The pilot program of RDT introduction to ADDOs in Kilombero, Kilosa, and Mvomero Districts trained 342 workers in 292 ADDOs to properly stock and perform RDT testing. The program conducted before and after intervention surveys. Results showed that 1) nearly half of people seeking treatment for fever in the intervention districts chose to test for malaria in the ADDOs, 2) most ADDO dispensers performed the test competently, 3) nearly all patients tested adhered to the recommended treatment

46

based on their test results and 4) the rational use of ACTs (i.e., the percentage of people taking an ACT only after receiving a positive test result) improved. These encouraging findings led to consensus between the MoHSW/NMCP TWG and various development and implementing partners, that the program should be scaled-up. The TWG formed a task force with a deadline of April 13th, 2015 to review pertinent policy and regulations and to produce a draft implementation plan for effective scale-up of RDT in ADDOs.

The protocol for the next therapeutic efficacy monitoring was approved in 2014 and preparations are underway to conduct the study at four sentinel sites in 2015 to assess continued in-vivo efficacy of ACT.

Zanzibar

To help improve RDT performance, ZAMEP in conjunction with partners conducted RDT QC in 146 health facilities and 190 testing sites in 2014. Sixty laboratory technicians (100% of those targeted for the year) received training in 2014 on basic malaria microscopy examination. Slides are collected on a monthly basis and 10% of negative and all positive slides were re-examined in a blinded manner by the ZAMEP laboratory. Significant quality improvement was noted with microscopy testing sensitivity increasing from 89.8% in 2012 to 97.8% in 2014. ZAMEP conducted quarterly supervisory visits to all district hospitals and health centers and held large stakeholder meetings to provide feedback to the districts about microscopy and RDT performance.

As mentioned above, the revised ZAMEP Diagnostic and Treatment Guidelines were finalized in April 2014. A total of 375 healthcare workers were trained between June and August 2014. Ongoing training with PMI support is expected to reach an additional 250 in 2015 and another 250 in 2016. Although the use of single-dose primaquine has been included in the guidelines it has not yet been operationalized as primaquine will need to be re-registered in Zanzibar. Once primaquine is registered, ZAMEP plans to train health care workers on its use and set up a system for detecting adverse drug reactions.

Commodity gap analysis

Table IVa: RDT Gap Analysis Mainland

Calendar Year	2015	2016	2017
RDT Needs			
Target population at risk for malaria	45,365,262	46,590,124	47,848,057
Total number projected fever cases	14,635,171	15,030,321	15,436,140
Percent of fever cases confirmed with microscopy	10%	10%	10%
Percent of fever cases confirmed with RDT	90%	90%	90%
RDT needs	13,171,654	13,527,289	13,892,526
Other RDT needs (wastage, QC, school outreach)	3,063,741	4,331,646	6,198,775
Total RDT Needs	**16,235,395**	**17,858,935**	**20,091,301**
Partner Contributions			
RDTs carried over (deficit) from previous year	0	4,105,430	894,320
RDTs from MOH	0	0	0
RDTs from Global Fund**	16,416,675	16,787,398	18,885,823
RDTs from Other Donors	0	0	0
RDTs planned with PMI funding	3,924,150	1,923,750	2,137,500
Total RDTs Available	**20,340,825**	**22,816,578**	**21,917,643**
Total RDT Surplus (Gap)	**4,105,430**	**4,957,643**	**1,826,342**

* Total population at risk and total projected fever cases obtained from HMIS. A projected population growth of 2.7% was applied.
** 2016 and 2017 Global Fund amount not yet approved, what have been shared is what have been submitted in Concept Note

Table IVb: RDT Gap Analysis Zanzibar

Calendar Year	2015	2016	2017
RDT Needs			
Target population at risk for malaria	1,487,890	1,528,063	1,569,321
Total number projected fever cases.	179,709	155,505	130,441
Active case detection (ACD)	53,079	71,067	89,055
Percent of fever cases confirmed with microscopy	10%	10%	10%
Percent of fever cases confirmed with RDT	90%	90%	90%
RDT wastage, QC and training (9%)	26,972	27,696	28,342
Total RDT Needs	**241,789**	**238,718**	**234,794**
Partner Contributions			
RDTs carried over (deficit) from previous year	0	373,486	552,869
RDTs from MOH	0	0	0
RDTs from Global Fund	0	418,100	0
RDTs from Other Donors	0	0	0
RDTs planned with PMI funding	615,275	0	0
Total RDTs Available	**615,275**	**791,586**	**552,869**
Total RDT Surplus (Gap)	**373,486**	**552,869**	**318,075**

Table Va: ACT Gap Analysis Mainland

Calendar Year	2015	2016	2017
ACT Needs			
Target population at risk for malaria	45,365,262	46,590,124	47,848,057
Total projected number of malaria cases	7,371,855	7,328,238	7,227,050
ACT needs in treatment	7,371,855	7,328,238	7,227,050
Other ACT needs (wastage, QC, maintenance of 9-15 MOS stock at MSD)	7,987,665	6,111,282	5,876,470
Total ACT Needs (in treatments)	**15,359,520**	**13,439,520**	**13,103,520**
Partner Contributions			
ACTs carried over (deficit) from previous year	0	0	0
ACTs from MOH	0	0	0
ACTs from Global Fund	7,623,840	9,945,245**	9,696,605**
ACTs from Other Donors	0	0	0
ACTs planned with PMI funding	1,742,460	912,847	1,825,695
Total ACTs (in treatments) Available	**9,366,300**	**10,858,092**	**11,522,300**
Total ACT Surplus (Gap)	**(5,993,220)**	**(2,581,428)**	**(1,581,220)**

*Total population at risk and total projected malaria cases obtained from HMIS. A projected population growth of 2.7% was applied.
** 2016 and 2017 Global Fund amount not yet approved, what have been shared is what have been submitted in Concept Note

Table Vb: Artesunate Gap Analysis Mainland

Calendar Year	2015	2016	2017
Artesunate Needs[1] (in vials)			
Target population at risk for malaria	45,365,262	46,590,124	47,848,057
Total projected number of severe malaria cases treated with artesunate	402,466	593,638	780,306
Total Artesunte Needs (in vials)	**1,298,089**	**2,164,991**	**2,985,284**
Partner Contributions			
Artesunate carried (in vials) over (deficit) from previous year	-	261,594	436,603
Artesunate (in vials) from MOH	0	0	0
Artesunate (in vials) from Global Fund	0	2,340,000	0
Artesunate (in vials) from Other Donors	0	0	0
Artesunate (in vials) planned with PMI funding	1,559,683	-	2,481,132
Total Artesunate (in vials) Available	**1,559,683**	**2,601,594**	**2,917,735**
Total Artesunate (in vials) Surplus (Gap)	**261,594**	**436,603**	**(67,549)**

[1]Total artesunate needs: This data has been obtained from quantification which takes into consideration IPD and OPD needs and the doses as per quantification table attached

Plans and justification

Mainland

Tanzania procures most but not all of its needed malaria commodities through the Global Fund. PMI will support the procurement of some malaria drugs intended for the public sector, specifically ACT treatments and injectable artesunate for the treatment of severe malaria.

PMI will continue to support procurement of RDTs and the scale-up and maintenance of nationwide microscopy and RDT testing accuracy QA/QC systems. The RDT QA/QC system relies on periodic supportive supervision performed by district and regional health teams and the training of those supervisors nationwide is in progress. Maintenance of this system will require ongoing financial support. PMI has fully funded the first phase of the National Malaria Slide Bank which is the foundation of the proposed microscopy external quality assurance system. FY 2016 funds will be used to collect additional slides and to support lab technician training.

Optimizing case management of febrile illness remains an ongoing challenge in Tanzania as it is throughout much of Africa. PMI intends to support improvement of both facility and community-based malaria case management with an emphasis on integration of service delivery with that for other major health priorities. To further improve community based case management and referral, with support from PMI the NMCP in collaboration with the MoHSW Community-based Health Care Unit and other partners intends to develop and pilot an integrated community case management (iCCM) strategy in line with the CBHPP in three selected districts. PMI funds will also be used to support the introduction of a QA system for case management of febrile illness.

Following the encouraging results of the pilot introduction of RDT services in ADDOs the MoHSW/NMCP is planning to support the introduction of RDT services in ADDOs once approved by the Pharmacy Council. Implementation will be primarily supported by the Global Fund with PMI funds being used to cover the financial gap. In addition PMI will provide support to the Pharmacy Council to develop its capacity to inspect and register ADDOs and to help the ADDO network develop a management unit that will strengthen the management and financial operations of target ADDOs and develop self-regulatory measures at a regional and national level. This will help inform the Pharmacy Council, which is responsible for managing the ADDO network and ensuring quality services.

Programmatic decisions regarding changes to malaria treatment policy require continuous data to demonstrate that first and second-line regimens remain effective at treating malaria parasitemia. Until molecular markers of resistance are identified, measurement and reporting of parasite clearance on day three after treatment with ACTs is particularly important, as this is one of the first signals of artemisinin resistance available today. PMI will support drug efficacy monitoring following the standard WHO protocol at four to five sentinel sites on the Mainland.

Zanzibar
As Global Fund support for FY 2016 has not yet been secured, PMI will plan to support procurement of RDTs for Zanzibar. PMI will also continue to support the maintenance of a flexible system to strengthen both RDT and microscopy performance and QA/QC at public facilities in Pemba and Unguja. This is primarily performed via monthly (microscopy) or quarterly (RDT) supportive supervision of health facility personnel. This QA/QC support will also include private health facilities.

ZAMEP has recognized a need for technical assistance to develop materials to facilitate health worker training on effective case management of malaria.

Proposed activities with FY 2016 funding: ($9,232,300)

Mainland
1. _ACT procurement to fill needs in the public sector._ The Global Fund is expected to procure most ACT needs on the Mainland. However, there remains a gap. Thus, PMI plans to procure 1.8 million ACTs to ensure no stockouts. _($2,000,000)_

2. *Artesunate procurement.* PMI will procure injectable artesunate (3 million vials) to fill the gap not covered by the Global Fund. *($1,600,000)*
3. *RDT procurement.* PMI will procure 2 million RDTS for public health facilities. *($1,000,000)*
4. *RDT and microscopy Quality Assurance and Quality Control.* PMI will support the maintenance and supervision of nationwide QA/QC systems for both RDT and microscopy. Funds designated for the NMCP will support additional supervisory staff as well as maintenance of the National Slide Bank. *($800,000)*
5. *Introduction of QA of fever case management.* These funds will be used to support the development/improvement of a QA system for case management of febrile illnesses. *($500,000)*
6. *Support for Integrated Community Case Management.* PMI funds will be used to support a pilot iCCM program in 3 districts *($250,000)*
7. *Support for improved management of febrile illness.* PMI will support facility-based provision of health services for improved diagnosis and treatment of febrile illness. *($1,921,300)*
8. *Scale-up of RDT introduction in ADDOs.* PMI will support the NMCP to scale-up introduction of RDT in ADDOs by covering some of the gap in Global Fund support. PMI will also provide support to the Pharmacy Council to develop its capacity to inspect and register ADDOs and help strengthen the ADDO network. *($500,000)*
9. *Routine therapeutic drug efficacy monitoring.* PMI funds will be used to support routine *in vivo* efficacy monitoring of artemether-lumefantrine and second-line treatments at four to five sites. *($250,000)*

Zanzibar

1. *RDT procurement.* PMI will procure approximately 360,278 RDTs for use in public health facilities. In addition, these supplies may be used for reactive case detection and response in the event of an unusual increase in reported cases identified through the MEEDS. *($200,000)*
2. *RDT and Microscopy Quality Assurance and Quality Control.* PMI will support the maintenance and supervision of QA/QC systems for both RDT and microscopy. This will include technical assistance to ZAMEP via the partner as well as direct funds to ZAMEP to support supervision and periodic feedback meetings to all districts about performance. *($120,000)*
3. *Technical meeting to develop case management guidance.* These funds will support technical meeting(s) to develop case management training materials including participant and facilitator manuals, treatment charts, and adverse drug reaction forms. Funds will support the printing of the materials. *($91,000)*

b. Pharmaceutical Management

NMCP/ZAMEP/PMI objectives

The NMCP objective for pharmaceutical management is to ensure an uninterrupted supply of quality malaria commodities throughout the Mainland and Zanzibar. Procurement and supply management on the Mainland and Zanzibar are supported by the Government of Tanzania, Global Fund, and PMI. The MoHSW has set minimum and maximum standards for stock availability at six and nine months, respectively.

Progress since PMI was launched

PMI supports the strengthening of the logistics system for ordering essential medicines, which includes ACTs, artesunate, and RDTs and is also working to improve the distribution system for essential medicines. In 2014 PMI supported End User Verification Surveys showed that there has been steady reduction in the percentage of facilities experiencing a stock out of antimalarials or RDT on the day of assessment but the issue of stock outs continues. In May 2015, EUV showed for the first time ever that at least one presentation of ACT was available at all facilities visited of a statistically representative sample. A combination of the ILS Gateway roll out, the new Logistics Management Unit, the eLMIS and having full supply of key malaria products at the national level have led to this reduction. Central Medical Store distribution processes continue to be a challenge and is one of the main causes for continued stock outs. PMI has co-funded the LMU's development of a Performance Monitoring Plan for key indicators including on-time delivery and order fill rate. It is felt that measuring these indicators and raising awareness of this performance will provide the LMU and other stakeholders to holding the Medical Stores Department accountable. On an annual basis, with support from PMI and other partners, NMCP, ZAMEP and MSD conduct quantification of malaria commodities and monitor the supply plan for the whole country. Bi-annual reviews are done to update stock tables and procurement plans. This exercise has assisted the MoHSW, NMCP, MSD, and the Pharmaceutical Services Section to manage the commodity pipeline for the country.

Progress during the last 12-18 months

Mainland
Through its supply logistics contractor, PMI procured 115,999 RDTs kits and 58,889 packs of ACTS for the Mainland in 2014. An additional 1,606,483 vials of artesunate are expected to arrive in May 2015. PMI supported the MoHSW to develop a Logistics Management Unit (LMU) which oversees all supply chain activities including malaria commodities. The LMU Charter was signed by the Minister of Health in 2014 and members of the LMU have had quarterly meetings with district pharmacists to discuss and address challenges. The unit has focal people at MSD central and zonal stores to better coordinate its requisition and supply system to healthcare facilities. They have also established a supply chain performance monitoring plan that allows them to hold key stakeholders including MSD accountable to a basic standard of service. Additionally, the electronic Logistics Management Information System (eLMIS) was rolled out to all districts in FY 2014.

Zanzibar
As on the Mainland, PMI provides support to ZAMEP in forecasting, quantification, and procurement planning for ACTs and RDTs. PMI supported the procurement of 7,680 RDTs for Zanzibar in 2014 and assisted ZAMEP with the establishment of their own Logistics Management Unit. A total of 15 staff positions have been allocated by the Ministry to the LMU and it will be operational beginning in July 2015. In addition, PMI has supported the development of a supply chain performance monitoring plan and rolled out end use verification programs. The Zanzibar-specific eLMIS was also rolled out to all districts during 2014. All of these activities were cost-shared with PEPFAR and other USAID health funds.

Plans and justification

To improve the procurement of needed commodities, PMI supports forecasting, quantification, and procurement planning for ACTs and RDTs and supports the MSD and MoHSW Pharmaceutical Supply Unit to institutionalize supply chain management functions. Support for malaria commodity logistics will continue to focus on monitoring the integrated logistics system to ensure continued availability of ACTs and other malarial commodities at health facility level. The logistics monitoring capacity of the district malaria/IMCI focal people will be strengthened and additional support provided on inventory control procedures at central, regional, and facility levels. A shift towards an emphasis on product availability accountability engaging local government authorities, specifically the RHMT and CHMT is expected in the next year. The Logistics Management Unit will continue to monitor their performance monitoring plan and target supportive supervision were performance in the supply chain is deemed poor.

The results-based financing (RBF) program, to be implemented in Kagera, will include supply chain performance indicators at MSD central and zonal store in Mwanza as well as at the facility level. This focus on outcome based incentives is intended to incentivize MSD to provide quality services. Tracer medicines included in the RBF scheme include all formulations of ACT and RDTs. PMI incentives to health facilities (75% of total) and individuals (25% of total) will be paid based on results that rely on both quantitative and qualitative indicators of performance. There is one direct malaria indicator being tracked by RBF, IPTp2+. Others are currently captured indirectly as part of incentives for supply chain, to ensure availability of medicines and medical supplies, including ACT and RDTs, and laboratory incentives to ensure a functional laboratory. PMI, the NMCP, and RBF are in agreement to introduce and pilot additional case management indicators as their component data points are added into the current routine Health Management Information System (HMIS). Examples include, a laboratory register that is being piloted in selected districts with the aim of being rolled out nationwide by the end of the calendar year, and a pharmacy dispensing register. Both will be fully integrated into the electronic HMIS database. The matched laboratory and clinical data will then be used to monitor the proportion of suspected malaria cases that are confirmed. NMCP will use this data to target their supportive supervision at the individual facilities and the RBF will use the increase in confirmed versus clinical cases as a diagnostic performance indicator.

Pharmaceutical and supply chain strengthening activities will also continue to include: conducting quarterly end-use verification surveys to a sample of health facilities and zonal warehouses to monitor the availability of key antimalarial commodities; visits to health facilities and regional warehouses to detect and respond to critical issues such as ACT (or other drug) stockouts; and establishing and strengthening systems for monitoring distribution of ACTs and RDTs from the Medical Store Departments to health facilities. Results from EUVs will be used to assess improvements in the logistics management and supply chain systems. PMI support will address medical waste management and final disposal, as per USG and local environmental laws.

In Zanzibar, PMI will support ZAMEP to collect consumption and logistics data needed for annual quantification and procurement planning, implement end-use verification surveys to monitor availability and use of malaria commodities at health facility level, and handle medical waste and final disposal of expired ACTs and RDTs.

Mainland
1. *Strengthen pharmaceutical management and supply chain system.* PMI will support improved quantification for RDTs and antimalarial drugs, transportation, storage, record keeping and will conduct End Use Verification surveys. *($750,000)*

Zanzibar
1. *Strengthen pharmaceutical management and supply chain system.* PMI will support improved quantification for RDTs and antimalarial drugs, transportation, storage, record keeping and will conduct End Use Verification surveys. *($100,000)*

5. Health system strengthening and capacity building

PMI supports a broad array of health system strengthening activities which cut across intervention areas, such as training of health workers, supply chain management and health information systems strengthening, drug quality monitoring, and capacity building for both the NMCP and ZAMEP.

NMCP/ZAMEP/PMI objectives

The health systems strengthening objectives are to ensure a sustainable, country owned, and integrated approach to malaria control activities. Despite the decline in malaria prevalence, the disease burden due to malaria remains considerable. By supporting health systems interventions, PMI and the Tanzania government aim to bolster the achievement of malaria control results and more importantly to sustain these gains as the country strives towards elimination of malaria. In particular, PMI funds have prioritized the following systems strengthening areas: 1) addressing critical health workforce shortages, 2) improving the availability of needed skills in the workforce to lead malaria control efforts, 3) reducing drug stockouts, 4) decreasing donor dependency for financing of malaria, 5) strengthening accountability and management of health care, and 6) improving data for decision-making.

Progress since PMI was launched

PMI support of health systems strengthening in 2006 initially focused on activities closely linked to malaria control, such as information systems strengthening for supply chain, institutional strengthening of planning capabilities of the NMCP and the ZAMEP, and capacity building of the National Bureau of Statistics to conduct major surveys like the DHS, SPA, and the THMIS. These efforts have resulted in the recent establishment of the country's first integrated electronic Logistics Management Information System detailing the availability and consumption of commodities, including those related to malaria, from all health facilities. The National Bureau of Statistics ability to lead its first THMIS (which demonstrated malaria prevalence decreasing to 9%) has increased country ownership, institutionalization, and use of routine nationally representative surveys to capture the burden of disease due to malaria. The success of the bureau's efforts has prompted the USAID Mission to enter into its first ever Government-to-Government health agreement with the bureau for such studies and begin to decrease international technical support over time.

Over the years, PMI has broadened its support of systems strengthening to address workforce shortages, and inadequate management and planning of health services and limited resources. Such efforts, co-funded with other USG funding sources (including funds for PEPFAR, maternal and child health, family planning/reproductive health, and tuberculosis), strengthened human resources planning, budgeting, financial management, and accountability at the local government authority level. These efforts influenced districts to integrate malaria in their comprehensive council health plans and as a result 70% of targeted health facilities now use their own cost-sharing funds to contribute to procuring malaria medicines and supplies. In addition, through introduction of health worker recruitment and retention strategies, vacancy rates in the Lake Zone (a targeted region for malaria control) dropped from 40% to 36%.

The African Field Epidemiology Network, the USAID Global Health Bureau, CDC-Atlanta and CDC-Tanzania (with PEPFAR funding) have all worked with PMI and PEFAR since 2007 to develop and strengthen the Tanzania Field Epidemiology and Laboratory Training Program (FELTP). FELTP is a public health training program to build competencies in applied epidemiology, implementation, evaluation, and management of disease interventions, surveillance strengthening, epidemic preparedness and response, and leadership skills. The program is managed by the MoHSW in collaboration with Muhimbili University of Health and Allied Sciences and National Institute of Medical Research.

During the two-year program, FELTP trainees are embedded within the MoHSW where they work daily with the staff of specific disease control programs (e.g., NMCP and ZAMEP). Residents have been conducting evaluations of malaria surveillance systems and planned studies on issues related to malaria and malaria diagnostics continuously since program inception. To date, there have been 5 graduating classes of 58 FELTP students, out of whom, 52 have been returned to government institutions and 6 are employed in the private sector. The fifth cohort of 13 trainees graduated in December 2014.

Since 2011PMI has supported Peace Corps in its fight against malaria as part of the Stomp Out Malaria campaign. Peace Corps Volunteers (PCV), working closely with the NMCP's implementing partners and other NGOs, focused on school net program awareness creation and behavior change activities, IRS-related data collection and analysis, management of trainings, as well as participation in World Malaria Day events.

Progress during the last 12-18 months
In the past 12 months, PMI's support of systems strengthening clearly impacted provision of high quality malaria services. A PMI partner supported the MoHSW to develop a Logistics Management Unit (LMU) which oversees all supply chain activities including malaria commodities. The LMU Charter was signed by the Minister of Health in 2014 and members of the LMU have had quarterly meetings with district pharmacists to discuss and address challenges. The unit has focal persons at MSD central and zonal stores to better coordinate its requisition and supply system to healthcare facilities. They have also established a Supply Chain Performance Monitoring Plan which allows them to hold key stakeholders including MSD accountable to a basic standard of service. Additionally, the electronic Logistics Management Information System (eLMIS) was rolled out to all districts in FY 2014, which will enable all districts to more accurately order and track supplies throughout the system. These three key achievements will reduce stock outs of crucial malaria commodities, which will enable facilities to provide continuous malaria prevention and treatment services in high priority regions.

Tanzania has an increasingly vibrant private sector and long history of engagement and collaboration for social impact in health and other development issues. Tea plantations and other agri-business companies have historically addressed malaria and now the Malaria Safe project has become a significant collaboration between many companies, the government and USAID. This past year, PMI funds were used to increase the number of companies engaged in Malaria Safe from 37 to 52. Malaria Safe works with employees, families, and communities by conducting malaria activities under four pillars: Protection (net, testing, medication), Education (employee family days, after work hour events), Visibility (malaria messages on labels/adverts) and Advocacy (recruiting other companies).

In the past 12 months, both the NMCP and ZAMEP have engaged in various activities to help them continue to build their capacity for malaria related work. This has included internal training and attending international conferences to present their work and keep abreast of the most recent evidence and work related to malaria control and treatment. Representatives from NMCP and ZAMEP attended the American Society of Tropical Medicine and Hygiene conference in November 2014, and gave presentations. NMCP staff gave an oral presentation on their IRS operation in the Lake Zone and ZAMEP staff presented on their surveillance activities focusing on the MEEDS and MCN. Internal trainings also help the staff to keep abreast of current knowledge. NMCP staff attended financial management training on managing USAID funds. ZAMEP staff are expecting to attend the following trainings in 2015: PCR training and RDTs low testing training (case management), M&E, stratification and electronic recording, accounting package and USAID financial management and regulations, health promotion, and mass media.

Peace Corps

PMI supports three Peace Corps Volunteers (PCV) who work very closely with the NMCP's implementing partners and other NGOs. PCVs focused on school net program awareness creation and behavior change activities, IRS-related data collection and analysis, management of trainings and events as part of a malaria curriculum called Malaria Skillz. During the past 18 months Peace Corps Volunteers and their counterparts provided education on malaria prevention through social behavior change communication messages, field practice, and use of mobile video unit (MVU) and school interventions strategies such as Pata Pata, the children's radio program. Peace Corps Volunteers were also engaged in World Malaria Day events and supported long-lasting insecticide treated bed net distributions and hanging demonstration events at clinics and aided in the distribution of malaria BCC materials. Peace Corps in collaboration with PMI, NMCP and malaria partners has successfully conducted two in-depth malaria trainings for new PCVs and their counterparts, 13 PCVs and 13 counterparts on programmatic implementation of the malaria programs in Tanzania. The training focused on current policy and implementation challenges in malaria prevention and case management, status of current malaria interventions in the Mainland and Zanzibar, and key priorities in the new National Malaria Strategic Plan.

Peace Corps participated in the Africa-wide The Malaria Hero Competition where Peace Corps Volunteers highlighted their counterparts who were doing especially inspirational work around malaria. In Tanzania a health PCV near Masasi nominated his counterpart, a village councilman and farmer, for his work in their village of Mkululu. The councilman helped to develop and implement a training of trainers at the ward level where one person from each village attended to learn about malaria science, prevention and treatment options. The long term goal was to provide human resources in each village that community members could seek out for issues related to malaria. For his work on this project, the councilman won the competition and was recognized by Peace Corps as the Malaria Hero. This year, Peace Corps Tanzania is having a Malaria Month Challenge where different regions compete to perform various malaria projects. The goal is to increase volunteer participation, and help volunteers effectively engage with their communities to approach malaria education and prevention in innovative ways.

Field Epidemiology and Laboratory Training Program (FELTP)

In the past 12 months, FELTP graduated its fifth cohort of residents and enrolled the seventh cohort since the program began in 2008. Residents have undertaken field placement assignments and conducted evaluations of various malaria activities including causes of blood infection among non- malaria febrile illness patient at Mnazi Mmoja Hospital in Zanzibar, patterns of malaria case management in children under five years of age at Misungwi District in Mwanza, evaluation of a sentinel surveillance system for monitoring malaria prevalence among pregnant women and infants at Reproductive and Child Health clinics (RCH) in Lake Zone, analysis of malaria laboratory data from three hospitals in Mwanza, Mara and Kagera Regions, and an evaluation of the MEEDS system and malaria data set analysis in Zanzibar. Residents made presentations at several conferences and all wrote dissertations.

Each trainee participates in several outbreak investigations in Tanzania, thereby developing their skills for future malaria outbreak investigations. Between 2013 and 2014 residents participated in ten outbreak investigations including one of malaria in Muleba District and another in Dar es Salaam that was initially diagnosed as malaria but proved to be an outbreak of dengue fever. The program organized two seminars facilitated by staff from PMI and NMCP on selected topics including malaria epidemiology and current trends, overview of various malaria data sources and surveillance systems, current policy and implementation challenges in malaria diagnosis and case management, status of current malaria interventions in the Mainland and Zanzibar, and key priorities in the new National Malaria Strategic Plan.

The CDC resident advisor is responsible for strategic planning for the program, and has assisted with mentoring these trainees and participates in classroom teaching (surveillance, study design, outbreak investigation, data analysis).

Plans and justification

This past year, the Tanzanian Mission received approval for its Country Development Coordination Strategy. This document prioritizes a holistic and integrated approach to achieving and sustaining results in alignment with broader development objectives. Indeed, as seen from the recent Singida results, a composite of HSS interventions across the WHO health system building blocks resulted in increased commodity availability rather than just a focus on addressing supply chain building block alone. Accordingly, PMI funds will be used to address underlying systems challenges to reaching and maintaining malaria results. Such an effort is critical to reaching and sustaining malaria elimination goals.

As such, PMI will co-finance efforts to target, through a single project mechanism, four WHO building blocks at both the national and district levels. Specifically, PMI funds will be used to 1) strengthen governance at the national and district levels to use resources transparently, to enable citizen engagement in planning and monitoring, and to produce results in health care, 2) increase domestic resources for health care as well as improve use of funds in terms of effectiveness, efficiency, and obtaining value for money, 3) improve equity in the distribution of health care workers providing quality essential health services, and 4) increase use of available data to inform decision-making processes at both the national and local levels. In addition, PMI will continue to strengthen the supply chain system, including the GoT's ability to better quantify, forecast, budget, monitor and ensure stock availability at the point of service delivery.

With FY 2016 funds, PMI will support two new systems strengthening areas. First, PMI will provide support for Tanzania's government led results based financing activity by supporting performance payments to facilities for provision of high quality malaria services and to supply chain actors for on time provision of key malaria commodities. Second, PMI will contribute to the GoT-led initiative to create an application that reaches down to the facility to allow for more frequent eLMIS reporting, with the eventual goal of having each facility able to monitor their stocks and make requests in real time rather than on a monthly or quarterly basis. This would greatly decrease the occurrence of stockouts and overstocks and complements, rather than duplicates, the data captured by the HMIS. PMI will also continue to support the NMCP and ZAMEP in capacity building activities.

Proposed activities with FY 2016 funding: ($1,898,000)

Mainland

1. *Capacity building for NMCP.* Strengthen capacity of NCMP by building up staff knowledge and skills via attendance at conferences, participation in short-terms trainings, study tour and other educational programs, other needs as determined by the training needs assessment currently being done by the NMCP. *($150,000)*

2. *Peace Corps Volunteers: BCC and Malaria Surveillance.* PMI will support three Peace Corps Volunteers ($10,000 each) to work with the NMCP and PMI implementing partners. PMI will provide funds Small Project Assistance grants ($10,000) that are available on a competitive basis to support PCVs' community-based BCC malaria activities. The funds will be spent on a ratio of 75% direct volunteer costs and 25% community based projects. *($40,000)*

3. *Support to FELTP Program.* PMI will continue support to the FELTP program and contribute to the advanced training of Tanzanian epidemiologists for a 12-month period. The trainees will receive assistance from resident advisors and participate in malaria field assignments and investigations throughout Mainland and Zanzibar. PMI will continue to track the placement of FELTP graduates into post-training MoHSW assignments that directly influence malaria control policies and practices. *($150,000)*

4. *Public Sector System Strengthening.* This project will holistically address systems issues associated with the building blocks of human resources for health, governance, finance and information use. Its geographic focus will be 13 regions on the Tanzania Mainland, inclusive of high prevalent malaria regions. PMI funds will be used for a number of HSS interventions including the implementation of the health care financing strategy, capacity building for public financial management at the district level, strengthening financial tracking in facilities to generate revenue, and joint planning and coordination across line Ministries and levels in the systems. These HSS interventions are critical to the success and sustainability of the malaria response. Finally, this project will instill the underlying systems, appropriate motivations, and checks and balances to eliminate malaria pharmaceutical stockouts at the facility level; i.e. with better planning and coordination on stock status, districts can avoid impending stockouts by using their discretionary funds to redistribute commodities from facilities with sufficient stock to those in need. *($450,000)*

5. *Results-based Financing (RBF).* RBF is a GoT-led project that provides performance payments to improve the quantity and quality of health services at dispensary, health center, district hospital, CHMT, and RHMT levels. The 17 quantitative indicators are all collected within the DHIS2, which over time improves data quality and promotes sustainability of the

approach. A quality checklist applied quarterly will be used to determine the final incentive paid to each facility, with 75% of the incentive used for facility level improvements and 25% distributed among employees. The RBF scheme also includes a supply chain component, which incentivizes MSD central and zonal units to improve indicators such as order fill rate, expired commodity rate, lead time, and on time delivery rate for artemether-lumefantrine 1x6, 2x6, 3x6, 4x6; SP; artesunate injection; and RDTs. The scheme has a strong verification component including internal verification by the Regional Administrative Secretary and other stakeholders, and external verification by the Controller Auditor General. Implementation will be supported by Public Sector Systems Strengthening and facility-based partners. RBF will specifically improve malaria prevention, case detection, and control by incentivizing household visits by CHWs (including messages on ITN use and linking sick household members to facilities), provision of IPTp, improvements in quality of care (including implementation of standard operating procedures for malaria testing and treatment), and availability of malaria commodities. *($683,000)*

6. *eLMIS phone application.* Currently, the eLMIS is only updated quarterly because of limited paper forms at the facility level. The GoT requested assistance to create an app that reaches down to the facility to allow for more frequent eLMIS reporting. The total cost of developing and implementing this app is $4 million, which includes the hardware costs and training of representatives in all of Tanzania's 6,000+ facilities. PMI funds will primarily contribute to the training component of the app roll out. Obtaining real time information on the stock status of bed nets and malaria treatment will allow the GoT and PMI to prevent stock outs and ensure facilities have the commodities necessary to prevent and treat malaria. *($300,000)*

Zanzibar

1. *Capacity building for the ZAMEP.* Strengthen capacity of the ZAMEP by building staff knowledge and skills via attendance at conferences, participation in short-terms trainings, study tour and other educational programs, and other needs as determined by the ZAMEP team *($110,000)*

2. *Establishment of Malaria Expert Committee.* PMI will support ZAMEP to establish a Malaria Expert Advisory Committee. This Advisory Committee will be made up of global malaria experts from the government, the donor community, and the private sector to provide high-level technical guidance to ZAMEP on how to reach the goal of achieving pre-elimination/elimination of malaria in Zanzibar *($15,000)*.

Table VI: Health Systems Strengthening Activities

HSS Building Block	Technical Area	Description of Activity
Health Services	MIP	Refresher trainings and integrated supportive supervision for MIP interventions in eight regions
Health Workforce	Case Management	Improve the distribution of human resources for health within high priority PMI regions to improve access to prevention and treatment services
	Case Management	Roll out community health worker cadre to high priority PMI regions to link communities to care and educate households on appropriate malaria prevention and care seeking behaviors
	Case Management	Support CHMTs to use human resource policies and practices to provide workers skilled in malaria prevention and treatment; support CHMTs in developing and financing context-specific retention packages
	Case Management	Introduction of QA system for CM of febrile illnesses
	Case Management	Introduction of RDTs in ADDOs
	FELTP	Support to FELTP trainees with focus on malaria
Health Information	M&E	Support GoT to ensure data is utilized by health providers and is accessible to clients to monitor and verify progress towards malaria targets; support evidence-based policy, investment and research decisions through access to timely, accurate and comprehensive reporting of malaria information
		Conduct baseline evaluation for public sector system strengthening activity to assess link between system strengthening efforts and malaria outcomes
Essential Medical Products, Vaccines, and Technologies	Pharmaceutical Management	Support improved forecasting, procurement, quality control, storage and distribution of malaria commodities, such as insecticide-treated nets, artemisinin-based combination therapies and rapid diagnostic tests; roll out eLMIS application to enable collection of real-time information on stock availability of key malaria commodities
		Support the Pharmacy Council to strengthen their management and financial operations.
Health Finance	Case Management	Provide technical assistance to leverage financial contributions and services from private sector partners for malaria prevention and control
	Health System Strengthening	Support LGA's prioritization and use of 'own source' health revenue collected at facilities to improve essential services, including malaria; support LGA's to effectively work around delays associated with the transfer of funds from the national government

Leadership and Governance	Health Systems Strengthening	Strengthen national coordinating and regulatory bodies to direct and manage malaria resources, develop guidelines, and improve quality of services; support LGAs to implement national level policies at the district level

6. Behavior change communication

NMCP/ZAMEP/PMI objectives

In order to achieve long-term change in the fight against malaria, both NMCP and ZAMEP focus on empowering individuals as well as addressing social and structural factors. In this regard, ZAMEP and NMCP communication strategies aim to build mutually supportive structures, systems and partnerships to empower individuals, families and their communities to take action in preventing malaria while at the same time provide an enabling environment that supports individual change and empowers service delivery structures.

The NMCP and ZAMEP BCC strategic plans aim to advocate for and communicate positive behaviors for malaria control. The BCC strategic plans serve as a guide to coordinate efforts, messages and activities for all malaria implementing partners. The Mainland BCC strategy has been updated to cover the period from 2014-2020 and aligns with the latest Malaria Strategic Plan covering 2012-2020. The Zanzibar BCC strategy covers the period from 2013-2018. The communication strategies address various aspects of healthcare around malaria prevention, treatment, and control. This includes high level political advocacy, local government level advocacy for planning, budgeting and coordination of malaria control interventions; service delivery to improve interpersonal communication and compliance to standards; and community and individual level improvements in demand, use, and compliance. The BCC strategies also target the media to create partnerships to advocate for and create awareness of malaria interventions. There is also an effort to engage the private sector through the Malaria Safe programs focused on encouraging private sector companies to invest in malaria through protecting their employees.

Progress since PMI was launched

PMI support of BCC activities has contributed to important findings. The 2011/12 THMIS reported that 92% of women knew a symptom of malaria, and awareness of malaria is universal at over 98%. Eighty-three percent of women and 91% of men had heard or seen the Malaria Haikubaliki (No More Malaria) slogan used on all malaria BCC in Tanzania, and 57% of women and 67% of men had heard or seen a malaria prevention message. The survey also found that women understand that pregnant women are at high risk of malaria (90%), that they could protect their children from malaria (82%), and that it was important to sleep under a net every night (93%).

Since inception, PMI has supported communication strategies for both Mainland and Zanzibar to address various aspects of health care around malaria prevention, treatment, and control including high level political advocacy; local government level for planning and budgeting for malaria control interventions; service delivery to improve interpersonal communication and compliance to standards;

and community and individual level improvements in demand, use, and compliance. BCC messages have also focused on the changing malaria situation in Zanzibar and in certain regions of the Mainland, such as the Lake Zone. Zanzibar BCC messages have focused on messages related to the continued risk of malaria despite reductions in prevalence and the need to be vigilant about malaria prevention and control activities.

PMI also supports efforts targeting the media to create partnerships to improve advocacy and awareness of malaria interventions, as well as engaging the private sector through Malaria Safe companies that aim to educate and engage their employees in malaria prevention and control efforts. PMI also partners with Peace Corps Volunteers who support the implementation of the Tanzania National Malaria Strategic Plan.

To date, PMI has supported the following activities/campaigns;

1). The Safe Motherhood Campaign that delivered malaria and other health messages to pregnant women, focusing on IPTp2 and ITN use during pregnancy.

2). The BCC component of the school-based net distribution program in the Southern Zone of Tanzania.

3). A new test-and-treat BCC campaign focused on getting healthcare workers to test all fevers. The slogan for this campaign is "Not all fevers are malaria, get tested".

4). Community mobilization through the Community Change Agent (CCA) platform. CCAs directly deliver messages to the community on ITN use; care of nets; testing, treatment, and dose completion; as well as malaria in pregnancy and IRS. They emphasize messages of increasing IPTp3+ and testing all persons with fevers.

Progress during the last 12-18 months

Mainland
Test and Treat Campaign
PMI funds supported the test-and-treat BCC campaign focused on getting people to test all fevers. This campaign was based on findings in the 2011-2012 THMIS that showed while malaria rates have been decreasing, the rate of fever has stayed the same. Thus the campaign slogan, "not all fevers are malaria, get tested" was developed. The campaign used broad messaging about getting treated if ill, as well as specific messaging promoting the use of RDTs in private sector clinics. The campaign included radio spots and print materials for the health facilities as well as outreach materials for community volunteers. The September 2014 Omnibus surveys showed that 52% of respondents had heard or seen the campaign. Of those, 67% could correctly identify the main message of the campaign to "get tested when you have a fever", and 40% said they knew they should "get tested when you think you have malaria". Evidence from a partner pilot project on RDT testing in ADDOs showed that the RDT wholesalers received more orders than anticipated in pilot areas which could signify a demand for the RDT with those districts. Also, controlling for other factors, regression results from the end line survey confirmed that those who were exposed to "not every fever is malaria" campaign messages in pilot districts were most likely to

test in ADDOs (p=0.015). One of PMI's partners together with NMCP has conducted formative assessment of phase one of the campaign and is finalizing development of phase two of the campaign.

Safe Motherhood Campaign

PMI continued to support the national integrated multimedia Safe Motherhood Campaign locally known as *Wazazi Nipendeni* (Love Me Parents) focusing on IPTp and ITN use during pregnancy. The campaign uses SMS platform to send weekly messages to service providers and health workers. Pregnant women and their supporters who subscribe to the service receive weekly reminders to go for antenatal care early, test for HIV/AIDS and go for prevention of mother to child transmission (PMTCT+) services, request SP for IPTp, and develop an individual birth plan. The campaign is monitored quarterly through Omnibus surveys, clinic data, and SMS registration reporting. The campaign channels include TV and radio messaging, provision of printed materials to over 3,000 clinics across the country including posters and SP reminder cards. The campaign also included messaging to pregnant women to request vouchers for ITNs. This was ended when the TNVS ended in June 2014. Messaging will be developed and disseminated once the new approach for distribution of ITNs through ANC clinics is established.

In November 2013, a post-hoc evaluation of the campaign was conducted, consisting of exit interviews at ANCs with pregnant women and women who had given birth within the last 6 months. The evaluation found that exposure to a large number of campaign sources had impact on increasing delivery at a health facility and sleeping under a net, while overall message exposure had influence on taking SP and knowledge about malaria prevention during pregnancy. The majority of surveyed women (60.2%) first visited ANC before reaching 16 weeks in their pregnancy – the recommended timing. The most frequently cited reason for delayed attendance among all respondents was that they did not see the need for attending the clinic so early in their pregnancy.

Moreover, a large percentage of women (69.8%) were aware of at least one malaria prevention strategy in pregnancy, and 89.3% of the total sample (N=1,708) reported owning a mosquito bed net. For each increase in message sources to which a woman was exposed, there was about a 61% greater likelihood the woman slept under a mosquito net the previous night, even controlling for all other demographic variables. Similar positive results were observed with regards to taking malaria prevention medications—the campaign had a significant impact on exposed women. The more message sources that women had been exposed to, there was about an 8% greater likelihood the woman received an SP dose. The more message sources women had been exposed to, there was about a 23% greater likelihood the woman received two or more SP doses.

The second phase of the campaign is currently underway with updated materials reflecting the IPTp3+ policy. Findings from phase one of the campaign have been used to inform messaging and campaign direction for phase two.

School Net Program (SNP)

PMI funds supported the BCC efforts for the second round of school-based net distribution program in the Southern Zone of Tanzania. This included the airing of promotional radio spots, 24 episodes on children's radio program, and print and promotional materials for the school children, schools, and community. The campaign accompanied the issuing of nets through the schools to a number of classes. Currently, evaluation of the second phase of SNP is being fielded and we expect results to be out by June 2015.

Malaria Safe Initiative

In 2014, PMI started to support the Malaria Safe initiative that was started under a Bill and Melinda Gates Foundation project. The project aims to engage private companies in promoting malaria prevention and control for their employees. The TCCP with NMCP is the secretariat for the initiative and the Minister of Health and Social Welfare is the Chair of the Steering Committee. This past year saw 15 new companies joining the initiative making the total active companies in the initiative to be 52. Malaria Safe companies educate their employees on malaria and provide nets to employees and their families. Last year, 256 peer educators from the Malaria Safe companies were trained. The companies also distributed 1,645 nets to their employees and they also send malaria prevention and treatment messages to about 3,786 employees across the 52 active malaria safe companies. Furthermore, a national Steering Committee was established and a framework for action developed and adopted by the companies. The NMCP has institutionalized Malaria Safe by including it as one of the main indicators for multi-sectorial component in the new Malaria Strategic Plan. The NMCP target is to have100 Malaria Safe companies by 2020.

Community Mobilization

PMI supported community mobilization in six regions last year. Through the Community Change Agent platform, 981,570 people were reached directly with messages on ITN use, care of nets, IRS, malaria in pregnancy, and malaria testing, treatment, and dose completion. The network was expanded to include all wards (837) in the districts and the Community Change Agents at the ward level identified two volunteers per village for all the villages in the ward, currently this includes 6,884 volunteers. These volunteers also have connections with the health facilities. Through this expanded network, the major focus is on increasing IPTp3+ and testing all fevers. In the six PMI supported regions, districts were able to allocate their own funding to support malaria BCC activities. PMI is assessing to see how much of the funding that was allocated by districts to support malaria BCC activities was actually disbursed; results are expected in July 2015.

Zanzibar

In Zanzibar, PMI has supported the BCC unit of the ZAMEP to operationalize the new communication strategy that aligns with the ZAMEP's new malaria strategy. The focus was on including BCC as one of the components of the active case detection response team. Thus, when the District Malaria Surveillance Officer is following up on a health facility reported case, they conduct a BCC sessions on malaria prevention and treatment with the index house as well as surrounding households. In addition, PMI supported the development of the new continuous distribution (CD) strategy for long-lasting ITNs. ZAMEP launched the CD strategy in June 2013. The selected channels for the CD strategy include EPI, ANC, active case detection and the community. Out of the annual target of 223,000 ITNs, 114, 394 nets have been distributed to community members as of December 2014. PMI provided technical assistance on the KAP study that was done in Zanzibar as a baseline to the CD. In October/November 2015, PMI will support an evaluation of the CD and findings will inform the ZAMEP decisions on Zanzibar's continuous distribution strategy.

Plans and justification

Mainland

BCC efforts will continue to focus on case management, malaria in pregnancy with IPTp3+ roll out, and school net distribution project in the Southern Zone. PMI will continue to support the Malaria Safe Companies Initiative with NMCP to facilitate the secretariat and to recruit new members. BCC efforts through mass media and interpersonal communication will also focus on engaging communities to work together to ensure households are accessing, using and caring for their nets as well as accessing health facilities for testing and treatment. For ANC visits, messages will focus on increasing use of IPTp through encouraging pregnant women to make sure they get at least three doses of SP and consistently sleep under an ITN during their pregnancy. Based on malaria stratification, BCC messaging and interventions will be tailored to respond to each region and district's unique situation. District leaders will also be targeted with BCC messages to encourage them to plan and budget for malaria prevention and control activities and to provide the human resources necessary to carry out these activities.

Media (regional and/or district level) activities such as radio and TV will be used to promote the above-mentioned areas, and their use will be dependent on the new malaria stratification maps that have been developed for the NMCP's Malaria Strategic Plan. Messages will be targeted to areas that are identified to receive those messages. High prevalence regions will get messages that differ in content than other lower prevalence areas. The intensity may change depending on the areas. This will also influence the expansion of the community mobilization component.

Now that NMCP has finished orienting health workers on the new SP 3+ policy, efforts will be made to target BCC messages to health service providers to overcome bias and barriers against SP provision, as well as using a quality improvement model at the clinic level to ensure that stock outs of SP and other malaria commodities become a rare occurrence. PMI will continue to support BCC in PMI focus regions. BCC efforts will support the SNP in the Southern zone with net use and care messaging and activities. In the mass distribution regions (Kigoma and Kagera), BCC efforts include working with community engagement as well as media. For IRS, BCC messages will be threefold. First, messages will continue to alert people to IRS being done in their districts/areas; a second set of messages will target places that are no longer a part of the IRS campaign to explain why; the third set will focus on addressing bed bugs, flies and other insects that appear after IRS. Messaging will focus on encouraging the community to accept the sprayers and having their homes sprayed, as well messages about the importance of using both spraying and net use together; previously these messages were separated.

Zanzibar

PMI will continue to support the BCC unit of the ZAMEP and the communication campaigns for continuous distribution of nets. New approaches to messaging for prevention will be identified to support policies developed by ZAMEP for returning travelers. Net use campaigns as well as the CD strategy will continue to be implemented with a focus on messaging for low transmission and pre-elimination as well as net care messaging. PMI will also continue to strengthen the capacity of ZAMEP BCC unit to work with the Active Case Detection team to ensure the BCC component is implemented

67

well and continues to engage and empower households with suspected malaria to take the steps necessary to protect the household members, to ensure testing when there is a fever, and to go to the clinic within 24 hours when there is fever. Based on the evaluation of the CD strategy in July/August 2015, PMI will support BCC efforts to support the later decided ITN replacement strategy, either CD or any mechanism that will be decided by ZAMEP and partners. PMI will also support a malaria school health intervention. The main aim is to provide health education to school children being key agents for change in the community. The School Health Program major objective is to sensitize school children to a range of health issues. ZAMEP is rolling out malaria prevention and treatment training and materials to teachers and school clubs in both Unguja and Pemba. This program is maintained through the school budgets, so funding in other years will be only to disseminate improved and updated malaria materials.

Proposed activities with FY 2016 funding: ($2,261,000)

Mainland
1. *ITN keep-up strategy:* Support to BCC to promote the scale-up of the school-based net program or alternative that the NMCP decides upon. Mass media is targeted to reach 75% of households in the SNP districts. Funding will be spent on radio (40%), print materials (20%), and community mobilization (40%). (*$350,000*)
2. *BCC for IRS:* Mobilize districts and communities, communicating change in IRS strategy, such as moving from blanket to targeted and to focal spraying, communicating changes in insecticide being used and addressing concerns about bed bug and flies after IRS. Funding will be spent on radio (20%), print materials (40%), and community mobilization (40%). (*$100,000*)
3. *Early malaria testing and treatment compliance:* To advocate for and mobilize service providers and communities for improved testing, compliance to malaria diagnostic and treatment guidelines, including seeking treatment within 24 hours of onset of fever. Funding will be spent on provider interpersonal communication and job aides (25%), radio (40%), and community mobilization (35%). (*$600,000*)
4. *BCC for IPTp3+:* BCC will be used to help continue the roll out of IPTp3+ with providers and pregnant women. The purpose of the campaign is two folds; create informed clients and to overcome providers bias and barriers. The money will support mass media, print materials, interpersonal communication skills and community mobilization activities. Funding will be spent on provider interpersonal communication and job aides (20%), mass media (50%), and community mobilization (30%). (*$550,000*)
5. *National level and Community Based Organizations coordination:* To better coordinate the efforts of various malaria BCC partners and ensure both consistency and harmonization of communication efforts, PMI will support NMCP to have a fully functional national level BCC working group and a vibrant BCC team that monitors what is going on in the districts as increasingly more district based activities are being implemented by CBOs. Funding will cover the cost for national meetings with CBOs implementing malaria BCC activities in respective district (70%) and supportive supervision for the NMCP BCC team (30%). (*$100,000*)
6. *Regional and district BCC coordination:* Based on a varying malaria situation in Tanzania, better BCC coordination is required at the lower level. PMI will support the NMCP to establish regional malaria BCC platforms/working groups that will be a forum to prepare and harmonize district-based malaria BCC plan with all partners at the district level. PMI will also work with NMCP to develop terms of reference for the district/regional based BCC working

group and orient regional and district teams to understand their roles and responsibility. Funding will be spent on orientation (40%), mentoring and support (30%) and facilitating first few meetings (30%). (*$300,000*)

Zanzibar

1.   *BCC support for multiple activities:* BCC for ITNs continuous distribution, BCC during active case detection, malaria diagnostic testing, adherence to treatment regimens, education and mobilization for outbreak response; and communicating insecticide rotation and IRS phase out. Funding will be spent on mass media (40%), print materials (40%) and community mobilization (20%). ($235,000)

2.   *School Health Program:* PMI will support 300 malaria school clubs to develop and print messages and sensitization of school pupils and parents/local communities on malaria messaging (ITN, IRS campaigns, etc). (*$26,000*)

7. Monitoring and evaluation

NMCP/ZAMEP/PMI activities
Epidemic Surveillance & Response
Mainland
The malaria risk profile is becoming more heterogeneous throughout the Mainland as malaria prevalence has decreased more in some regions than in others. True malaria epidemics are uncommon, but seasonal increases in transmission do occur. Thus, the Mainland is working towards developing a sustainable Malaria Early Epidemic Detection System (MEEDS) that can detect sudden increases in transmission. The NMCP's principal objectives for epidemic surveillance are: 1) to attain 100% reporting of key malaria indicators from all districts, 2) to establish a MEEDS in areas of unstable transmission to detect 100% of malaria epidemics within one week of onset, 3) to effectively respond to malaria epidemics within two weeks of detection, and 4) to strengthen monitoring and evaluation of malaria control interventions, activities, policies, and strategies.

Zanzibar
PMI continues to focus attention and resources to epidemic surveillance and response activities in Zanzibar which is in the pre-elimination phase. In FY 2008, PMI provided technical and financial support to the ZAMEP to develop and implement MEEDS. The system includes a strategy to collect daily data for three key indicators (total visits, confirmed malaria-positive cases, confirmed malaria-negative cases) among outpatients visiting peripheral health facilities. Weekly aggregated data, stratified by age, are transmitted from each health facility using a customized cell phone menu. All data is received by a computer server operated by a Tanzanian telecommunications company. The weekly data is processed by the server and packaged into two useful formats: 1) text messages with weekly data summaries sent to cell phones of key ZAMEP staff and district medical officers; and 2) longitudinal weekly data made available for viewing over a secure web site.

Zanzibar instituted a malaria case notification (MCN) system at the end of 2011 with the aim of conducting a household investigation of every confirmed case of malaria infection within 24 hours of notification from the health facility where the case was diagnosed. In this system, the District Malaria Surveillance Officer (DMSO) travels to the case household to interview and test household members and occasionally those of neighboring households when specific hotspots are identified and investigated. While there, the DMSOs provide BCC materials on the need for early testing and adherence to treatment. They ascertain ITN use and provide coupons for a free net as needed. They also identify visible larval sources and provide information on environmental management.

Monitoring and Evaluation (M&E)

Mainland
The NMCP's objectives for M&E in addition to the above epidemic surveillance objectives are: 1) to attain 100% reporting of routine and periodic key malaria indicators from all districts 2) to strengthen and expand the scope of the M&E malaria indicators collected periodically, including intervention coverage, quality of service provision, parasite prevalence, vector susceptibility and dynamics, therapeutic efficacy of medicines, and availability of quality assured commodities and 3) to develop a comprehensive framework for collecting and storing malaria impact, outcome, and output data from programmatic monitoring and periodic surveys including nationwide household surveys and sentinel surveillance in pregnant women and school-aged children.

Nationwide (Mainland and Zanzibar)
The NMCP receives a large amount of data from its own M&E activities and those of multiple national and international malaria partners. For several years, PMI has been supporting efforts to: 1) strengthen the data management unit within the NMCP to store, analyze, and disseminate information for decision making, 2) hold regular meetings to discuss M&E activities, and 3) make regular M&E supervisory visits to the field. PMI will continue to support these activities.

PMI has worked closely with colleagues from the NMCP, the ZAMEP, Global Fund, WHO, World Bank, Malaria Control and Evaluation Partnership in Africa, other units of the MoHSW (e.g., HMIS, Integrated Disease Surveillance and Response (IDSR), and Health Sector Reform), and other sectors of the Government of Tanzania (National Bureau of Statistics, Ministry of Education) to promote coordinated M&E efforts.

The following data sources and timelines provide the foundation for PMI's and the Government of Tanzania's evaluation of malaria control outcomes and impact.

Demographic and Health Surveys (DHS). Every four to five years, the DHS collects nationally representative, population-based data for a wide variety of demographic and health indicators, including core malaria intervention coverage indicators, anemia, and all-cause under-five child mortality. It is conducted by the National Bureau of Statistics (NBS) with technical assistance from partners. NBS is currently finalizing survey instruments for the 2015 survey and the results are expected to be out by early 2016.

Malaria Indicator Survey (MIS). The MIS survey assesses core household coverage and morbidity indicators used in Tanzania. In 2007 and 2011, PMI co-funded the first and second population-based MIS combined with an AIDS Indicator Survey (THMIS). The 2011-12 THMIS survey results were officially released in March 2013 and provided critical data for NMCP/PMI's effort to evaluate the impact of malaria control efforts (see *Progress on Coverage and Impact Indicators section* for results). The main benefit to malaria is that with the larger AIS funding and sample size, regional level data were obtained for parasitemia (as with HIV prevalence) without an added cost. However, new PEPFAR requirements will now mandate more intensive sampling that will preclude combining the AIS and MIS. Therefore the MIS will be combined with the DHS in 2015/16. The survey is currently in the final stages of preparing the survey instruments and pretesting. The MIS results are expected to be released before the end of 2015

Health Management Information System (HMIS/ DHIS2). The objectives of the HMIS/DHIS2 are to provide data for monitoring key process, outcome, and impact indicators over time: 1) standardized laboratory-confirmed malaria cumulative incidence per year, among patients under five years old, patients older than five years, and pregnant women; 2) IPTp uptake among pregnant women; and 3) standardized crude laboratory-confirmed malaria death rate among patients under five years of age, patients older than five years, and pregnant women. Historically, the majority of malaria cases reported to this system represented clinical diagnoses, usually non-specific fever. However, this situation is changing as Tanzania continues to scale up the use of RDTs at health facilities of all levels. HMIS information is reported annually through Council Health Management Teams and the Health Statistics Abstract. Data flows from the health facility level up to the central level, where it is compiled, analyzed, and reported. Currently, a major multi-donor initiative (including PEPFAR) is reforming the existing paper-based HMIS platform to the electronic DHIS2. When fully implemented this is expected to reduce duplicate facility level data collection, reporting and entry. PMI staff continues to ensure that malaria is well represented in the ongoing DHIS2 implementation plans.

Integrated Disease Surveillance and Response (IDSR). IDSR captures data on notifiable/epidemic-prone diseases which are reported on a daily, weekly or monthly basis depending on the disease. Three malaria data variables are captured in the IDSR– total tested (RDT/microscopy), total positive, and total treated clinically. The long term strategy for IDSR is to use mobile phone technology for data submission (eIDSR) and this has been piloted in 12 districts across four regions using PMI support and seven districts were covered by MoHSW. The eIDSR uses an Unstructured Supplementary Service Data (USSD) application to transmit data to DHIS2 platform for subsequent analysis, and reporting.

Implementing Partner Reporting System (IPRS). Effective performance monitoring is critical to PMI success in achieving results. Since 2010, PMI has relied on the Implementing Partner Reporting System (IPRS) as the USAID/Tanzania Mission's source of data for PMI Annual Reporting. IPRS is a web-based system where PMI implementing partners enter their performance data on a quarterly basis which is then certified by the A/COR. A new award, Monitoring, Evaluation and Learning Program (MELP) will continue the support and implementation of IPRS and incorporate its function into a Mission wide database. MELP will also provide support in data quality assurance for key indicators, and provide data analysis to improve decision making, planning and implementation of malaria activities.

Monitoring and Evaluation Strengthening Initiative (MESI). This is an ongoing activity, led by the Government of Tanzania and supported partially by PMI, aimed at strengthening the Health Management Information System (HMIS) to better collect, manage, and report health data.

End-Use Verification Surveys (EUV). This is a public health facility supply chain monitoring activity to assess the performance of the public health supply chain, focused first on malaria commodities. The activity provides key information regarding the availability of these products, as well as visibility into how malaria is being diagnosed and treated at the health facility level. Tanzania was the pilot country for the EUV in Jan 2009, and has continued to implement the activity on a quarterly basis since that time. Supply chain information is captured not only for malaria commodities, but also for other essential medicines and reproductive health commodities.

Entomologic monitoring. Three categories of routine entomologic monitoring have been supported by PMI on the Mainland and Zanzibar:

1. Insecticide resistance monitoring of products used for vector control (once per year at national sites, selected from a network of 22 sites, on the Mainland and a total of 12 sites for Zanzibar)
2. Cone bioassay monitoring of residual insecticidal activity on sprayed walls (every 4-9 weeks on the mainland and at monthly intervals in Zanzibar)
3. Monitoring of vector species abundance and distribution, resting behavior and sporozoite rates at established sentinel sites both on the mainland and Zanzibar

Progress since PMI was launched

Mainland
Monitoring and Evaluation
PMI support for M&E and survey related activities started in 2006 and focused on the following areas: 1) the Health Management Information System (HMIS) and routine services statistics, 2) Demographic and Health Surveys (DHS), 3) Malaria Indicator Surveys (MIS), 4) Service Provision Assessments (SPA), 5) Integrated Disease Surveillance and Response (IDSR), 6) the Implementing Partner Reporting System (IPRS), 7) the Monitoring and Evaluation Strengthening Initiative (MESI), 8) End-Use Verification Surveys (EUV) , 9) Entomologic monitoring, 10) supporting Malaria Program Review (MPR) and 11) Impact evaluation.

Among the PMI supported surveys are the Tanzania HIV and Malaria Indicator Survey (THMIS 2007-08, 2011-12) and 2015 DHS/MIS which was launched in July 2015. Performance monitoring has been a PMI priority to ensure that data collected and reported by implementing partners are of high quality to inform management decisions. This has been realized through supporting routine data quality assessments of all PMI indicators and financial support to manage the IPRS which is a web based information system where PMI partners enter program data on a quarterly basis. This system has been a source for Tanzania PMI reports. In 2012 PMI also supported the SPA which was implemented in FY 2014.

In 2010 Tanzania was the first PMI focus country to carry out an in-depth evaluation of the impact of the scale up of malaria prevention and treatment measures on childhood mortality. This evaluation was conducted in collaboration with the Government of Tanzania, the Roll Back Malaria (RBM) partnership, WHO and the Ifakara Health Institute.

In 2011, the NMCP, in collaboration with partners, undertook a comprehensive review of the progress and performance of the malaria program for the period of 2002 to 2011.The MPR identified gaps which the NMCP has been working to address. The next MPR is planned to be conducted in 2017

In 2013, PMI supported a pilot of the electronic IDSR (eIDSR) in 12 districts and the plan is to roll out to the rest of the districts across 4 regions. These weekly reports will be important in monitoring of malaria control efforts especially in regions where malaria prevalence is declining.

Entomologic monitoring
The national resistance monitoring on the Mainland, supported by PMI through its implementing partner NIMR Amani Research Center, currently consists of 22 sentinel sites from 22 regions in the Mainland. These include PMI IRS districts in the regions of Mara, Mwanza, Geita, and Kagera Regions. These sites were selected based on areas with high malaria prevalence, history of insecticide use (both for public health and in agriculture) in the area, level of ITN coverage, demography (urban/rural) and site accessibility.

The NIMR-Mwanza entomology facility, serving as a regional entomology center for the Lake Victoria basin, conducts routine entomologic monitoring of PMI-supported IRS activities in the districts. Monthly mosquito collections performed by the regional/district health authorities are sent to NIMR-Mwanza for processing and analysis from a total of five sentinel sites in Geita, Mwanza, and Mara Regions. In addition, cone wall bioassays are conducted to monitor residual insecticide activity of the insecticide used for IRS. In 2010, when IRS was expanded in Mwanza, Geita and Mara Regions, entomologic monitoring was correspondingly expanded and currently there are four sentinel sites to cover the IRS regions.

Zanzibar
Monitoring and Evaluation

PMI has been supporting surveillance activities in Zanzibar such as the MEEDS (passive surveillance) and the Malaria Case Notification (MCN) system of active malaria case notification and follow-up.

Since inception, PMI has continued to support and strengthen several monitoring and evaluation activities for Zanzibar:

- The Malaria Early Epidemic Detection System (MEEDS) is designed to identify and enable a rapid response to increases in malaria transmission. Health facility-based early epidemic detection sites now exist in 214 sites, consisting of all government health facilities in Zanzibar and some of the larger private facilities. This system has already detected several small outbreaks which triggered investigations.

- The Malaria Case Notification (MCN) system was implemented at the end of 2011 with the aim of conducting a household investigation of every confirmed case of malaria infection within 24 hours of notification from the health facility where the case was first detected. Screening for malaria parasites is currently done for index case household members and for residents of nearby households.

- An Impact Evaluation was conducted in Zanzibar for which the full report will be released before the end of 2015. The preliminary results in Zanzibar show that the scale-up and maintenance of high vector control coverage and availability of antimalarial treatments have contributed to keeping malaria parasitemia prevalence below one percent between 2007 and 2012 and contributed to the eight-fold decline in confirmed malaria incidence in children under five years of age between 2005 and 2010. Likewise, hospital admissions for malaria have fallen from 30-50% of all admissions in 2000 to about 5% in 2012. Malaria deaths accounted for approximately half of all hospital deaths in 2000, but no confirmed malaria deaths have been reported since 2009. These achievements in malaria control are enabling Zanzibar to move towards malaria elimination.

Entomologic monitoring

From 2005 – 2012 the ZAMEP conducted longitudinal entomologic monitoring in four sentinel sites in Unguja and three in Pemba. Analysis of the MEEDS data from 2009-2012 indicated areas of persistent malaria transmission. In November 2013, entomologic monitoring was expanded from 4 sentinel sites in Unguja to 12 sentinel sites to evaluate these areas of persistent malaria transmissions. Similarly in Pemba the entomologic monitoring sentinel sites were expanded from three to ten sites. This provides information on vector species and density, human blood feeding index and malaria infection rates in the various vector species. In addition, the ZAMEP also conducted IRS monitoring activities such as residual efficacy testing and insecticide resistance monitoring. The ZAMEP conducts wall contact bioassays to monitor the efficacy the insecticide used in the, using their colony of susceptible *An. gambiae s.s.* The ZAMEP continues to conduct yearly insecticide resistance monitoring in both islands at five sites each on Pemba and Unguja.

Progress during the last 12-18 months

Mainland
Monitoring and Evaluation
The basic HMIS/DHIS2 system has been successfully rolled out countrywide as of December 2013. PMI supported the successful pilot of the eIDSR system in 12 districts across four regions of Tanzania through its implementing partner and will continue to support the rollout to facilities in the Lake Zone and eventually in other regions. PMI also supported a one-year pilot of sentinel population malaria surveillance among pregnant women and infants in the Lake Zone.

The NMCP, in conjunction with the Wellcome Trust/KEMRI and Ifakara Health Institute, has developed a Malaria Epidemiologic Profile which it will use to better focus malaria control efforts. The Malaria SME Strategic Plan is nearing finalization and should be disseminated before the end of 2015. With PMI support, the NMCP has reconstituted the Surveillance, Monitoring & Evaluation technical working group and held the first meeting of the wider SME network. The TWG will be convened to formally discuss and approve the Strategic Plan. After that, it is expected that the TWG will begin to meet regularly beginning in late 2015.

With FY 2012 funds, PMI contributed $450,000 to support the second national facility-based survey—the Tanzania Service Provision Assessment (SPA). The survey was implemented in October 2014 and data analysis is ongoing. Preliminary report is expected by May 2015. These findings will provide information at regional level on the availability, readiness, and quality of malaria and other health and HIV/AIDS services at the regional level.

PMI supported the integration of malaria indicators into the electronic IDSR surveillance system and its piloting in 12 districts across four regions of Tanzania. As it is still not fully operational continued reliance on paper-based reporting will continue until the system is fully rolled out. In addition to the new malaria prevalence indicators in the HMIS/DHIS2, NMCP in collaboration with the HMIS unit has developed the new HMIS Laboratory and Dispensing registers to capture both diagnosis and consumption data in health facilities. The tools have been piloted in 25 health facilities of Kibaha District and NMCP is expecting to roll out the tools countrywide staring in May 2015. The HMIS unit has added new indicators to better quantify at the health facility level the number of patients with a positive malaria test who are dispensed antimalarial drugs. Data from DHIS has been available since November 2014.

PMI has identified Tanzania as a site for the pilot routine information system strengthening activity. The main objective is to improve malaria data quality and use within the HMIS in order to monitor changes in malaria burden over time and inform program planning. Use of these data will ultimately strengthen national programs and improve health outcomes. This activity is being implemented in three phases including: 1) Planning, 2) Implementation, and 3) Evaluation. During the first phase malaria data quality problems were identified, prioritized and a work plan was developed for addressing the problems in a collaborative manner with all stakeholders. The second phase, implementation, will be done in collaboration with the MoHSW. The pilot for the implementation project will be conducted in Pwani region in August and September of 2015.

Along with other USAID health programs PMI is co-funding with FY 2014 funds midterm and end-of-project evaluations of the management of febrile illnesses project (Tibu Homa) in Lake Zone and the Tanzania Capacity and Communication Project behavior change communication program (TCCP). The statements of work for these evaluations have been completed and are in the process of procurement. Findings from these evaluations will inform future programmatic planning. The TCCP evaluation is ongoing and evaluation findings will be available by end of May 2015. While the Tibu Homa midterm evaluation was not conducted due to reasons beyond program reach, the endline evaluation is scheduled to take place in August 2015. The scope of work for this evaluation is under review.

An evaluation of the second round of the school net program in Ruvuma, Lindi and Mtwara began in April 2015 and results will available by the end of 2015. The evaluations following the first and second SNP distribution used household based random cluster surveys. The first evaluation provided promising indications of success in maintain ITN coverage.

Entomologic Monitoring
In 2014, the NMCP received funding from the Global Fund to set up a national entomology surveillance program in their Malaria Surveillance Framework as part of their Malaria Strategic Plan 2014-2020. The NMCP worked with the Local Government Authorities and the Local District Councils to select 62 sentinel districts. Each district will have two sentinel sites where monthly longitudinal entomologic surveillance for mosquito densities, species composition and malaria infection rates will be carried out. To date, two Vector Control Officers in each of 62 councils have completed a two-week entomology training program. The NMCP plans to implement the surveillance program by the mid-2015.

NIMR-Amani has a total of 22 sentinel sites for insecticide resistance monitoring. In 2014, the national insecticide resistance monitoring program carried out insecticide resistance testing in 18 of the 22 sites using the WHO standard assay for permethrin, deltamethrin, bendiocarb and lambdacyhalothrin at all 18 sites.

Results are presented for all sites with a lower than 98% mortality. Permethrin resistance, ranging from 10% to 55% was detected in 3 of the 18 sites. Two sites indicated possible permethrin resistance, between 6.7 and 7.5%. Lambdacyhalothrin resistance was more widespread and was found in 11 of the sites (11% - 62%) and one site indicated possible lambdacyhalothrin resistance at 6.7%. Deltamethrin resistance was detected in six sentinel sites (14.4% - 41%) and possible resistance in five sites (2.2% - 8%). Resistance to at least 2 of the pyrethroids was detected in 9 of the 18 sites. Bendiocarb resistance was detected in 1 of the 18 sites (41.8%) and possible resistance in 2 other sites (6.7% and 7.5%). In PMI IRS regions, the insecticide sentinel sites were the districts of Geita, Magu, Musoma, and Ngara. In Magu and Ngara lambdacyhalothrin resistance was detected at 23.7% and 16.7% respectively. In Geita reduced susceptibility was detected for deltamethrin and lambdacyhalothrin (resistance at 3.3% and 6.7%). In Musoma there was also reduced susceptibility to permethrin; resistance was at 5%. There was no bendiocarb resistance in any of the PMI IRS regions.

The mosquitoes used in these tests were identified to species by molecular assays. Seventy-eight percent of the mosquitoes used in these tests, across the 18 sites were *An. arabiensis*. This indicates an increasing predominance of *An. arabiensis*. In 2005, routine entomologic data shows that before the scale-up of interventions in 2005, *An. arabiensis* made up 4% of the mosquitoes collected. In addition the mosquitoes were tested for the *kdr* insecticide resistance mechanism by molecular assays and enzymatic resistance mechanisms were tested using biochemical assays. East *kdr* mutations were detected in five of the sites, two of which included PMI IRS sites of Musoma and Ngara. Enzymatic resistance assays conducted in five sites show elevated esterase and glutathione –s-transferase activity that affect pyrethroid and DDT susceptibility. No enzymatic resistance evaluation was carried out in any of the PMI IRS regions.

Monitoring of the pirimiphos-methyl CS residual efficacy of the IRS in the Lake Zone was conducted in five sentinel sites, one in Geita Region, two in Mwanza Region and two in Serengeti region. The cone bioassays using susceptible *An. gambiae s.s.*, from the NIMR-Mwanza facility were tested on different wall surfaces sprayed with pirimiphos-methyl CS (mud, cement, painted and wood). Residual efficacy monitoring of pirimphos-methyl CS monitoring in the Lake Zone of the eighth spray campaign of 2014 indicated that all wall types retained >80% residual efficacy up to six months post-spray. After six months there were differences in efficacy between the wall surfaces between the sites. For example at the Geita site, mud and wood walls retained their >80% residual efficacy for seven months whereas cement and painted walls maintained efficacy up to six months post-spray. However, in Sengerema site all wall surfaces retained >80% efficacy for seven months post-spray.

Currently entomologic monitoring for vector species is being carried out in the three IRS districts with a total of five sentinel sites: Geita/Chato in Geita Region, Sengerema and Ukerewe in Mwanza Region, and Serengeti and Rorya in Mara Region. In 2014, light traps and clay-pot traps continued to be used for monthly collections. Between October 2013 – April 2014 PCR species identification was carried out for mosquitoes collected from the five sentinel sites as well as from two previous sentinel sites in Kagera

Region (Muleba and Karagwe) and another site from Mara (Tarime). The changes in sentinel sites reflect the changes in areas where PMI implemented IRS in 2014. Of 1,777 *Anophelines* collected at the eight sites between October – April 2014, 58.9% were from the *An. gambiae* complex (30.7% *An. gambiae s.s.*, and 28.2% *An. arabiensis*) and 41.1% were from the *An. funestus* complex (31.4% *An. rivulorum*, 8.9% *An. parensis*, 0.7% *An. funestus s.s.*). There were variations in vector species composition between regions. In the Kagera and Geita Regions, predominantly mosquitoes from the *An. funestus* complex were collected (40.8% of total collected) and only 0.5% were from the *An. gambiae* complex. In the Mwanza and Mara Regions, mainly mosquitoes from the *An. gambiae* complex were collected (58.5%) with *An. funestus* family complex making up 0.7% of the collection from these areas. 3,330 mosquitoes were processed for ELISA and 50 (1.5%) were found to be positive for *P. falciparum*. The highest *P. falciparum* infection rate was found in mosquitoes collected from Geita Region 3.7% (13/347 mosquitoes) and the Mara region 2.03% (9/442 mosquitoes). Mwanza Region had an infectivity rate of 1.2% (20/1614 mosquitoes).

Zanzibar
Epidemic response
As of 2015 the MEEDS system covers a total of 214 reporting sites, consisting of all 154 government and 60 private health facilities in Zanzibar . The ZAMEP is planning for eventual expansion to the remaining 14 private health facilities. A data quality assessment showed that the completeness of reporting has reached 100% with 95% of weekly reports being submitted by Friday. There is >90% agreement between MEEDS and HMIS data. The ZAMEP recommends the addition of at least one DMSO to specific districts such as West, Central and North B which tend to have larger numbers of cases particularly during peak transmission seasons.

In 2014 a total of 4,137 cases of malaria were reported in Zanzibar, an increase of 26.4% compared to 2013. Of these, 3,147 were detected through passive surveillance at health facilities and the remaining 990 through active surveillance via the MCN system and focal screening and treatment. Of the 3,147 cases identified through passive surveillance, 2,574 (82%) were investigated by DMSOs via the MCN. Through this case investigation, a total of 13,487 household members were tested for parasitemia and 763 (6.0%) who tested positive were treated with ACTs. Fifty-one percent of the 3,147 cases reported travel outside Zanzibar within the prior month, indicating that a substantial number of infections were likely acquired outside of Zanzibar. The overall functioning of the MCN is good with 51% of cases notified within 24 hours and 82% of cases followed-up at the household level. The ZAMEP disseminated information about the functioning of the MEEDS and MCN to the districts via quarterly reports. Using data from the MCN, the ZAMEP has initiated village mapping to highlight foci of transmission (hotspots) in relation to implementation of various interventions.

Because of very low rates of asymptomatic parasitemia detected during large-scale reactive case detection conducted in prior years, the ZAMEP has revised their epidemic response guidelines to focus reactive case detection efforts ; on family/household members of notified cases (household screening and treatment). Villages where cases detected within a week are >=5 (Highly focal; screening and treatment for the entire village) and *shehias* where cases detected within a week are >=10 (Focal: screening and testing for the entire *shehia*).

Monitoring and Evaluation

PMI is supporting an evaluation of the Zanzibar ITN continuous distribution approach, launched in June 2014. The channels for distribution include ITNs delivery through ANC and EPI clinics, community-based systems, and to households during follow-up visits to the homes of each malaria cases. The evaluation is proposed for late 2015 and will identify strengths and challenges to this new approach in Zanzibar.

Entomologic Monitoring

In 2014, the WHO conducted two rounds of insecticide resistance testing in Zanzibar: the first between April-June and the second between October-December.

Insecticide resistance testing was performed at a total of nine sites on Pemba for permethrin, deltamethrin, lambdacyhalothrin, alpha-cypermethrin, bendiocarb and pirimiphos-methyl CS. Insecticide resistance testing was carried out at three sites in Unguja for the same insecticides except that deltamethrin and lambdacyhalothrin were not tested in Unguja. The mosquitoes identified to species and were also screened for target site mutations of insecticide resistance mechanisms (*kdr*).

In Pemba, resistance was detected for all five sites monitored for lambdacyhalothrin (23% - 66%), for six sites monitored for permethrin (25% - 51%), for two sites for deltamethrin (51%-57%) and three sites for alpha-cypermethrin (60% - 67%). No resistance was detected for bendiocarb or pirimiphos-methyl CS. In Unguja, resistance was detected at one site tested for alpha-cypermethrin (12%), and in one site for permethrin (61%). There was no insecticide resistance detected for bendiocarb or pirimiphos-methyl CS. The continued widespread pyrethroid resistance in Unguja and Pemba, in spite of rotation with two IRS spray rounds with bendiocarb followed by two rounds of pirimiphos-methyl CS, per WHO recommendations for insecticide resistance mitigation, is concerning. This situation should be monitored closely as this may impact the efficacy of long-lasting ITNs. In Pemba, 93% of the mosquitoes used in the evaluations were *An. arabiensis*, 1% was *An. gambiae* and 1% was *An. merus*. In Unguja however 44% were *An. arabiensis,* 49% were *An. gambiae* and 6% were *An. merus*. A total of 1,015 mosquitos from the insecticide resistance evaluations were tested for *kdr* resistance mutation and none were found to be *kdr* positive.

Residual efficacy of pirimiphos-methyl CS was monitored monthly using the WHO cone bioassay with different wall surfaces (mud, oil painted, water painted, lime washed, un-plastered cement, and un-plastered stone blocks). Two- to five-day old susceptible *An.gambiaes.s.* mosquitoes from the insectaries in Pemba and Unguja were used. Residual efficacy of pirimiphos-methyl CS in Pemba and Unguja indicated that efficacy was maintained at >80% up to seven months post spray. After eight months post spray, the residual efficacy decreased on all surfaces except of oil-painted surfaces.

In 2014 sentinel site monitoring continued the expansion begun in late 2013 in order to evaluate sites of persistent transmission despite improvements in coverage of malaria control interventions. Ten sites were monitored on Pemba and 12 in Unguja. This expansion will be evaluated and the number of sentinel sites will be determined based the most recent epidemiological and entomological data.

Vector abundance is linked with the rainy season and is bimodal. The highest densities are in April-June corresponding to the long rains. There is an increase in mosquito populations during the short-rains between November-December. In Pemba the man landing collections indicate that 91% of the mosquitoes were collected out-doors and Unguja 55% of the mosquitoes were collected outdoors.

There has been a shift in vector species composition and vector dynamics on both islands since 2005. *An. arabiensis* continues to be the predominant vector in Pemba, with increasing numbers of *An. gambiae s.s.* collected in Unguja. Man landing collections in Pemba continue to show that transmission is occurring mainly through outdoor biting, a pattern consistent with the predominance of the more exophilic and exophagic *An. arabiensis*. However in Unguja, biting is now occurring both indoors and outdoors and this may reflect the increase in *An. gambiae*. Since 2011, *An. funestus* was also detected in some parts of Unguja, for example in Mwera.

Blood meal analysis of engorged mosquitoes collected from pit-traps and pyrethrum spray collections from Pemba showed that 72% of these mosquitoes feed on bovines, 8% on humans and 20% fed on other animals. No blood fed mosquitoes were collected in Unguja in 2014. A total of 1,506 mosquitoes were tested for *P. falciparum* infections, 7 of which were found to be positive. In Pemba, two of the positive *An. arabiensis* were from the Tumbe sentinel site which is one of the persistent malaria hot-spots. The other five positive *An. arabiensis* were from Unguja, Bumbwini and Donge Mchangani. To date, molecular identification of the mosquitoes has been outsourced to partners such as the CDC and IHI. PMI is supporting the implementation of a molecular laboratory at ZAMEP. The molecular analysis for mosquito speciation will be transitioned to ZAMEP when the molecular laboratory is implemented at ZAMEP in June 2015, which will support both epidemiological and entomological activities.

Table VII. Monitoring and Evaluation Data Sources

Data Source	Survey Activities	Year								
		2010	2011	2012	2013	2014	2015	2016	2017	2018
National-level Household surveys	Demographic Health Survey (DHS)						X	X		
	Malaria Indicator Survey (MIS)		X				X		X	
Health Facility and Other Surveys	SPA survey			X						
	EUV survey					X	X			
Malaria Surveillance and Routine System Support	MEEDS (Zanzibar)		X	X	X	X	X	X	X	X
	Integrated Disease Surveillance and Response (IDSR)		X	X	X	X	X	X	X	X
Therapeutic Efficacy monitoring	*In vivo* efficacy testing	X	X	X	X	X	X	X	X	X
Entomology	Entomological surveillance and resistance monitoring		X	X	X	X	X	X	X	X
Other Data Sources	Malaria Impact Evaluation	X				X				

Plans and justification

Mainland
The core of the routine malaria surveillance system is the HMIS/DHIS2 and the IDSR. In conjunction with other donors, PMI is supporting the strengthening of these two platforms and the implementation of the electronic reporting system which is expected to substantially reduce the time delays NMCP has experienced in receiving, analyzing, and acting upon the data. In addition to data from the routine surveillance system the NMCP receives reports and data from a wide array of their own M&E activities, plus ongoing activities in other parts of the MoHSW, sentinel surveillance sites, and from all PMI-funded partners. Data flow and utilization of these data need to be improved. PMI support will strengthen the data management unit within NMCP to collect, store, analyze, display, and disseminate information for decision making.

PMI will continue to support and evaluate the Mission-wide M&E services contract which covers a broad range of M&E services such as: 1) performance monitoring (via a web-based reporting system), 2) M&E Capacity Building, and 3) Data Quality Assessment and Evaluation. The web-based performance monitoring system will collect and store data before reporting and includes all required PMI reporting indicators. Implementing partners enter performance data quarterly and upload their narrative reports that serve as data sources.

Tanzania has changed its guidance to reflect the WHO recommendation that IPTp-SP should be provided to all pregnant women at each scheduled ANC visit after the completion of the first trimester. However, given the potential risks associated with use of IPTp-SP in areas with highly resistant parasites, monitoring for the development of these resistant parasites is crucial. With FY 2014 funding PMI proposed to monitor the prevalence of resistance markers against SP in parasites recovered from pregnant women attending first ANC visits at the sentinel sites that were part of the OR study to monitor malaria parasitemia among pregnant women and infants. The study has been approved by the local IRB and implementation has already started in the Lake and Southern Zones of Tanzania, the final report is expected to be completed by the end of August 2015.

Zanzibar
PMI will support the maintenance of MEEDS at all government and private health facilities. Refresher training and supportive supervision visits for diagnostics and surveillance will be increased. PMI will continue to support reactive case detection among household and neighborhood contacts of confirmed cases. Epidemic confirmation procedures will be maintained and response systems further strengthened to allow the ZAMEP to deploy a small cadre of trained staff to investigate all suspected epidemics.

Proposed activities with FY 2016 funding: ($4,623,500)

Epidemic Surveillance and Response ($1,248,000)

Mainland

1. *Support for continuation of eIDSR rollout.* The MoHSW has begun rollout of the eIDSR

with plans to cover 5 regions in 2014 with an additional 5 to 10 regions in 2015. In 2016 the roll out will cover 5-10 regions, and the remaining regions 5-10 will be covered in 2017, depending on the progress in 2016.*($500,000)*

Zanzibar

1. *Maintain MEEDS, MCN and outbreak preparedness/response. ($748,000)* PMI will continue to support passive surveillance through MEEDS and active surveillance through malaria case notification (MCN) and household screening and treatment (HSaT). Funds will be used to maintain malaria epidemic preparedness and response. Potential responses include: reactive and proactive case detection through focal or mass screening and treatment; mass treatment of fever cases in the affected community; focal IRS; and supplies for management of both uncomplicated and severe malaria. Response activities will require coordination with other interventions to ensure availability of buffer stocks and periodic rotation of commodities.
    - *IT support to maintain data communication for MEEDS and MCN ($70,000)*
    - *Support case follow up and investigation (case-based response) ($256,000)*
    - *Support to DRT (event-based response) ($200,000)*
    - *Maintain and strengthen data use and dissemination ($222,000)*

Monitoring and Evaluation ($2,336,000)

Mainland

1. *Routine System Strengthening.* PMI will continue support the RSS activity to improve malaria data quality and use within HMIS in order to monitor changes in malaria burden over time and inform program planning. Use of these data will ultimately strengthen national programs and improve health outcomes. *($200,000)*

Zanzibar

1. *Disseminate evaluation of delivery of ITNs to pregnant women and infants.* Feedback meeting with implementers and partners involved in continuous distribution *($12,000)*

Mainland and Zanzibar
1. *Support for Malaria Indicator Survey.* PMI will provide support to the 2017-18 MIS. This study will help to evaluate the ITN Malaria Replacement Campaign (MRC), will include malaria prevalence biomarkers and will provide critical outcome and impact data. *($1,500,000)*
2. *Integrated supportive supervision.* PMI will support the NMCP and ZAMEP to oversee integrated supportive supervision. Funds will also be used for coordination of Technical Working Groups (TWGs) for all interventions supported by ZAMEP and NMCP. *($310,000)*
3. *Implementing Partner Reporting System (IPRS).* PMI will continue to support the IPRS through the new USAID Mission wide award M&E project Monitoring, Evaluation and Learning Program (MELP) as the central data collection point for all implementing partners. Funds will also be used to support data quality assessments of key malaria indicators and providedata analysis.*($294,000)*
4. *Technical assistance for M&E.* CDC staff will conduct two TA visits to assist with

strengthening of malaria surveillance and other monitoring activities, including technical expertise in malaria program reviews, national and special surveys, and routine health information systems. *($20,000)*

Entomologic Monitoring ($1,039,500)

Mainland

1. *Entomologic monitoring.* This includes longitudinal monitoring in the Lake Region, insecticide resistance monitoring at 22 national sentinel sites, and WHO bioassays to monitor insecticide residual efficacy. Certain sites will be selected for testing each year, such that each site will be tested once every two years. This will provide a database of insecticide resistance and efficacy for the NMCP and other partners. *($650,000)*
2. *Quality Assurance for the national entomological surveillance at 62 district councils.* This surveillance activity will be funded by Global Fund. PMI support will be to provide oversight for all activities from mosquito field collection, sample processing/analysis in the laboratory to data collection and information quality. PMI expects to have periodic reports from NMCP on the results from the Global Fund supported 62 entomological monitoring sites. Of the 62 new sites, 3 will be located in districts where PMI supports entomological monitoring. PMI will work with NMCP to ensure that these new cites are not in close proximity to the existing PMI sites.*($100,000)*

Zanzibar

1. *Entomologic monitoring.* PMI will continue support to the ZAMEP in entomologic monitoring including insecticide resistance testing, longitudinal monitoring and insecticide bioefficacy evaluations and laboratory processing of mosquitoes at ZAMEP. The number of longitutinal monitoring sentinel sites will be capped at 14, with the final decision on the number of sites to be based on the latest entomological and epidemiologica data. PMI will continue to assist the ZAMEP in developing its molecular laboratory capability for entomological and epidemiological monitoring and surveillance. *($171,000)*
2. *PCR-based entomologic monitoring.* PMI will support operational costs, maintenance, fuel for generator. This will cover PCR for both entomology and diagnostic work. *($25,000)*
3. *Procurement of laboratory supplies.* PMI will support the transition of procurement of laboratory supplies, reagents and consumables for molecular and immune-diagnostic laboratory analysis of samples from epidemiologic and entomologic activities *($40,000)*

Mainland and Zanzibar

1. *Procurement of entomological reagents.* PMI will continue to support procurement of entomology supplies and laboratory reagents for the insectary, testing mosquitoes for malaria parasites, and for insecticide resistance testing that are difficult for Tanzania to source in-country. *($10,000)*
2. *Technical assistance for entomological monitoring.* CDC staff will conduct three TA visit to support entomological monitoring for Mainland and Zanzibar. To provide technical assistance to NIMR Mwanza to achieve the necessary routine entomologic monitoring of post spray activities and to monitor the entomology effects of the under five coverage campaign and the UCC in non-IRS area. In Zanzibar CDC will provide technical assistance to increase ELISA

capability to include blood meal analysis for vector biting preferences and essays for mosquitoes. *($43,500)*

8. Operational research

Strategy

Development of a national malaria operational research agenda is underway and will include essential research initiatives to guide the strategic plan implementation and provide evidence for innovative initiatives. The agenda and the identified operational research priorities will form the bases for resource mobilization. A provisional research priority list is presented in the National Malaria Strategic Plan 2014-2020 and includes research on outdoor biting, insecticide resistance, chemoprevention, introduction of a malaria vaccine, interaction of ACTs and antiretrovirals, and therapeutic efficacy studies.

The Effectiveness of Non-Pyrethroid Insecticide-Treated Durable Wall Liners as a Method for Malaria Control in Endemic Rural Tanzania: *Cluster Randomized Trial*

This is a multi-year study led by the National Institute of Medical Research (NIMR) Amani Centre with administrative support from TRAction. This study is funded primarily by PMI core funds, with additional support for ITN procurement provided by PMI Tanzania. The original study design called for a three-arm cluster randomized trial to assess the protective efficacy of a DWL with two non-pyrethroid insecticides plus ITN, ITNs plus IRS, and ITNs alone. The study was put on temporary hold to allow for an external team to intensively review the study and make recommendations for improvements. As a result the study has been revised to remove the IRS arm in favor of a two-arm study of DWL plus ITN vs ITN alone and the age of the incidence cohort was extended from 6-59 months to up to 11 years old. Participants will be tested for malaria monthly. The study is on track to begin after the start of the long rainy season in September/October 2015. Distribution of ITNs and installation of the DWL will occur in July-August 2015. In addition to the primary outcome of malaria, testing will be done for anemia and lymphatic filariasis and a cost-effectiveness analysis will be performed

Determining the effect of holes of different sizes and varying concentrations of insecticide in bednets on personal and community protection using Pyrethroid resistant and Pyrethroid susceptible *Anopheles gambiae*

This study was approved by the OR Working Group in 2014 and will be implemented by the Swiss Tropical and Public Health Institute and Ifakara Health Institute using MOP FY 2014 funds. The study will explore the relationship between net damage, remaining insecticide, and feeding inhibition in susceptible and resistant vectors in hut trials. The results will help to define a) the cut-offs to be used to determine "end of useful life" and b) how the cut-offs need to be adjusted with increasing vector resistance. The study will look at the determinants of net entry for local malaria vectors, in order to better advise industry on ITN design, and provide data useful to behavior change campaigns (BCC) on net care for Afro-tropical countries with malaria transmission by susceptible *Anopheles arabiensis* and resistant populations of *Anopheles gambiae s.s.*

Placental parasitemia among women who have not had intermittent preventive treatment (IPTp) for malaria in Zanzibar

Zanzibar conducted a placental parasitemia study among women who had not had IPTp for malaria. The goal of this study was to measure placental parasitemia rates among pregnant women delivering in the selected facilities in Zanzibar who had not received IPTp and to provide cost-benefit analyses to help inform policy decisions on the IPTp program in Zanzibar; the study results were published in 2014[12] and served as the basis for the ZAMEP decision to discontinue IPTp in Zanzibar.

Table VIII. PMI-funded Operational Research Studies

Completed OR Studies			
Title	**Start date**	**End date**	**Budget**
Placental parasitemia among women who have not had intermittent preventive treatment (IPTp) for malaria in Zanzibar	08/2011	09/2012	$122,150
Ongoing OR Studies	**Start date**	**End date**	**Budget**
Title			
The effectiveness of non-pyrethroid insecticide-treated durable wall liners as a method for malaria control in endemic rural Tanzania: *Cluster randomized trial*	07/2013	08/2016	Core-funded
Determining the effect of holes of different sizes and varying concentrations of insecticide in bednets on personal and community protection using pyrethroid resistant and pyrethroid susceptible *Anopheles gambiae*	03/2015	02/2016	$162,918
Planned OR Studies FY 2016			
Title	**Start date (est.)**	**End date (est.)**	**Budget**
No studies planned with FY 2016 funding			

9. Staffing and administration

Two health professionals serve as resident advisors to oversee PMI in Tanzania, one representing CDC and one representing USAID. In addition, three Foreign Service Nationals (FSNs) work as part of the PMI team. All PMI staff members are part of a single interagency team led by the USAID Mission Director or his/her designee in country. The PMI team shares responsibility for development and implementation of PMI strategies and work plans, coordination with national authorities, managing collaborating agencies and supervising day-to-day activities. Candidates for resident advisor positions (whether initial hires or replacements) will be evaluated and/or interviewed jointly by USAID and CDC,

---

[12] http://www.ajtmh.org/content/91/2/367.long

and both agencies will be involved in hiring decisions, with the final decision made by the individual agency.

The PMI professional staff work together to oversee all technical and administrative aspects of PMI, including finalizing details of the project design, implementing malaria prevention and treatment activities, monitoring and evaluation of outcomes and impact, reporting of results, and providing guidance to PMI partners.

The PMI lead in country is the USAID Mission Director. The day-to-day lead for PMI is delegated to the USAID Health Office Director and thus the two PMI resident advisors, one from USAID and one from CDC, report to the USAID Health Office Director for day-to-day leadership, and work together as a part of a single interagency team. The technical expertise housed in Atlanta and Washington guides PMI programmatic efforts.

The two PMI resident advisors are based within the USAID health office and are expected to spend approximately half their time sitting with and providing technical assistance to the national malaria control programs and partners.

Locally-hired staff to support PMI activities either in Ministries or in USAID will be approved by the USAID Mission Director. Because of the need to adhere to specific country policies and USAID accounting regulations, any transfer of PMI funds directly to Ministries or host governments will need to be approved by the USAID Mission Director and Controller, in addition to the US Global Malaria Coordinator.

Proposed activities with FY 2016 funding: ($2,360,000)
PMI will support salaries and travel costs of two PMI Resident Advisors, two FSN PMI Project Management Specialists, the M&E Officer, and support office (OAA, OFM, and the Program Office) staff. Total management and administrative costs, excluding the salary and benefits of the USAID and CDC PMI Resident advisors and locally employed PMI staff is approximately 2% of the total budget.

USAID administrative and technical support. ($1,700,000)

CDC administrative and technical support. ($660,000)

Table 1: Budget Breakdown by Mechanism

President's Malaria Initiative – TANZANIA

Planned Malaria Obligations for FY 2016

Mechanism	Geographic Area	Activity	Budget ($)	%
TBD-Vector Control Mechanism	Lake Zone and South	ITN keep-up program	7,010,000	15.6%
TBD – Supply Chain Contract	Lake Zone and South	ITN keep-up program	5,500,000	12.2%
TBD – Supply Chain Contract	Zanzibar	ITN keep-up program	830,000	1.8%
TBD - Supply Chain Contract	Mainland	ACT procurement	2,000,000	4.4%
TBD - Supply Chain Contract	Mainland	Injectable artesunate	1,600,000	3.6%
TBD - Supply Chain Contract	Mainland	RDT procurement	1,000,000	2.2%
TBD - Supply Chain Contract	Zanzibar	RDT procurement	200,000	0.4%
TBD - Supply Chain Contract	Mainland	Strengthen pharmaceutical management and supply chain system	750,000	1.7%

TBD - Supply Chain Contract	Zanzibar	Strengthen pharmaceutical management and supply chain system	100,000	0.2%
ZAMEP	Zanzibar	ITN keep-up program	185,200	0.4%
ZAMEP	Zanzibar	Technical meeting to develop CM guidance	91,000	0.2%
ZAMEP	Zanzibar	Capacity building	110,000	0.2%
ZAMEP	Zanzibar	Expert Committee to help ZAMEP move towards pre-elimination	15,000	<0.1%
ZAMEP	Zanzibar	School Health Program	26,000	0.1%
ZAMEP	Zanzibar	Entomological and insecticide resistance monitoring including PCR	236,000	0.5%
ZAMEP	Zanzibar	Maintain Malaria Early Epidemic Detection System (MEEDS) reporting and outbreak preparedness/ response	526,000	1.2%
ZAMEP	Zanzibar	BCC across all interventions	235,000	0.5%
ZAMEP	Zanzibar	Integrated supportive supervision	160,000	0.4%
ZAMEP	Zanzibar	Dissemination of findings of continuous net distribution evaluation	12,000	<0.1%
IRS 2 TO6 (AIRS)	Lake Zone	IRS for Mainland and Zanzibar	8,750,000	19.4%
IRS 2 TO6 (AIRS)	Zanzibar	IRS for Mainland and Zanzibar	500,000	1.1%

IRS 2 TO6 (AIRS)	Mainland	National insecticide resistance & intensity monitoring; longitudinal monitoring and IRS bioefficacy in the Lake Zone	650,000	1.4%
IRS 2 TO6 (AIRS)	Mainland	Entomological monitoring QA for 62 sites	100,000	0.2%
TBD - Facility Based Mechanism	Mainland	Continued support for MIP in 4 regions and expansion to 4 new regions	1,000,000	2.2%
TBD - Facility Based Mechanism	Mainland	RDT & Microscopy strengthening including QA/QC system	600,000	1.3%
TBD - Facility Based Mechanism	Zanzibar	RDT & Microscopy strengthening including QA/QC system	120,000	0.3%
TBD - Facility Based Mechanism	Mainland	Introduction of QA fever management	500,000	1.1%
TBD - Facility Based Mechanism	Mainland	iCCM pilot	250,000	0.6%
TBD - Facility Based Mechanism	Mainland	Management of Febrile illness to children of under 5 years	1,921,300	4.3%
TBD - Facility Based Mechanism	Mainland	Therapeutic drug efficacy monitoring	250,000	0.6%
NMCP	Mainland	RDT & Microscopy strengthening including QA/QC system	200,000	0.4%
NMCP	Mainland	Capacity building	150,000	0.3%
NMCP	Mainland	Integrated supportive supervision	150,000	0.3%

TBD	Mainland	Scale-up of RDT in ADDOs	500,000	1.1%
TBD	Mainland	e-LMIS phone application to expand eLMIS to facilities	300,000	0.7%
PS 3	Mainland	Finance, HRH, Governance HSS national and LGA level	450,000	1.0%
World Bank	Mainland	Results-based Financing (RBF)	683,000	1.5%
Peace Corps	Nationwide	Peace Corps	40,000	0.1%
TBD - BCC Mechanism	Mainland	BCC across all interventions	2,000,000	4.4%
TBD - Surveillance Mechanism	Mainland	Support of eIDSR	500,000	1.1%
TBD - Surveillance Mechanism	Zanzibar	Maintain Malaria Early Epidemic Detection System (MEEDS) reporting and outbreak preparedness/ response	222,000	0.5%
TBD - Surveillance Mechanism	Mainland	Routine System Strengthening	200,000	0.4%
TBD - MELP	Nationwide	Program database management and data quality assurance	294,000	0.7%
ICF Macro	Nationwide	Malaria Indicator Survey (MIS)	1,500,000	3.3%
CDC	Nationwide	Continued support to FELTP	150,000	0.3%
CDC	Nationwide	Procurement of entomological supplies	10,000	<0.1%
CDC	Nationwide	Technical Assistance Entomological Monitoring	43,500	0.1%

CDC	Nationwide	Technical Assistance for M&E	20,000	<0.1%
USAID	-	Administrative USAID	1,700,000	3.8%
CDC	-	Administrative CDC	660,000	1.5%
Total			**$45,000,000**	**100%**

Table 2: Budget Breakdown by Activity

President's Malaria Initiative – TANZANIA

Planned Malaria Obligations for FY 2016

Proposed Activity	Mechanism	Budget		Geographic Area	Description
		Total $	Commodity $		
PREVENTIVE ACTIVITIES					
Insecticide-treated Nets					
ITN keep-up program	TBD - Supply Chain Contract	5,500,000	5,500,000	Lake Zone and South	Procure 1,665,000 ITNs for distribution to pregnant women through ANC clinics and to school children through SNP in the South and Lake Zones
ITN keep-up program	TBD - Vector Control Mechanism	7,010,000	-	Lake Zone and South	Support for logistic and management of delivery of ITNs through ANC and SNP in seven regions of Tanzania
ITN keep-up program	TBD - Supply Chain Contract	830,000	830,000	Zanzibar	Procurement of 251,758 bed nets
ITN keep-up program	ZAMEP	185,200	-	Zanzibar	Support for logistics and management of distribution including transportation and warehousing
SUBTOTAL ITNs		13,525,200	6,330,000		

Proposed Activity	Mechanism	Budget		Geographic Area	Description
		Total $	Commodity $		
Indoor Residual Spraying					
IRS for Mainland and Zanzibar	IRS 2 TO6 (AIRS)	8,750,000	2,625,000	Lake Zone	To support targeted IRS in the Lake Zone reaching approximately 350,000 structures and protecting about 1.5 million people. This includes insecticide, PPE, training, waste collection, spraying, and enforcement of regulations.
		500,000	150,000	Zanzibar	To support focal IRS in hot spots covering about 70,000 HH/people. This includes insecticide, PPE, training, waste collection, spraying, enforcement of regulations.
SUBTOTAL IRS		9,250,000	2,775,000		
Malaria in Pregnancy					
Continued support for MIP in 4 regions and expansion to 4 new regions	TBD - Facility Based Mechanism	1,000,000	-	Mainland	Support integrated training and supervision of ANC staff to ensure proper implementation of ITPp3+ and case management of MIP
SUBTOTAL MIP		1,000,000	0		
SUBTOTAL PREVENTIVE		23,775,200	9,105,000		

CASE MANAGEMENT

Proposed Activity	Mechanism	Budget		Geographic Area	Description
		Total $	Commodity $		
Diagnosis & Treatment					
ACT procurement	TBD - Supply Chain Contract	2,000,000	2,000,000	Mainland	Funding for approximately 1.8 million ACT treatments
Injectable artesunate	TBD - Supply Chain Contract	1,600,000	1,600,000	Mainland	PMI will procure 3 million vials of injectable artesunate to fill gap not covered by GF
RDT procurement	TBD - Supply Chain Contract	1,000,000	1,000,000	Mainland	Procure approximately 2 million RDTs for public health facilities
		200,000	200,000	Zanzibar	Procure approximately 360,000 RDTs for public health facilities, reactive case detection, and outbreak use
RDT & Microscopy strengthening including QA/QC system	NMCP	200,000	-	Mainland	Support to NMCP for supervisory staff as well as maintenance of the National Slide Bank as part of nationwide diagnostics QA/QC system
	TBD - Facility Based Mechanism	600,000	-	Mainland	Maintenance and supervision of nationwide QA/QC system for RDTs
	TBD - Facility Based Mechanism	120,000	-	Zanzibar	Support the maintenance and supervision of QA/QC systems for both RDT and microscopy. This will include technical assistance to ZAMEP via the partner as well as direct funds to ZAMEP to support supervision and periodic feedback meetings to all districts about performance

Proposed Activity	Mechanism	Budget		Geographic Area	Description
		Total $	Commodity $		
Introduction of QA fever management	TBD - Facility Based Mechanism	500,000	-	Mainland	Support for facility-based provision of health services for improved diagnosis and treatment of febrile illness
iCCM pilot	TBD - Facility Based Mechanism	250,000	-	Mainland	Support for the pilot of an iCCM program in three districts
Management of febrile illness in children under five years of age	TBD - Facility Based Mechanism	1,921,300	-	Mainland	Support for facility-based provision of health services for improved diagnosis and treatment of febrile illness
Scale-up of RDT in ADDOs	TBD	500,000	-	Mainland	Training, supervision, and quality assurance; support to the Pharmacy Council to strengthen the ADDO network
Therapeutic drug efficacy monitoring	TBD - Facility Based Mechanism	250,000	-	Mainland	ACT efficacy monitoring of 4 sites
Technical meeting to develop CM guidance	ZAMEP	91,000	-	Zanzibar	Support technical meeting(s) to develop case management guidelines and develop and print supporting materials
Subtotal Diagnosis & Treatment		**9,232,300**	**4,800,000**		
Pharmaceutical Management					
Strengthen pharmaceutical management and supply chain system	TBD - Supply Chain Contract	750,000	-	Mainland	Strengthen quantification, distribution, storage, inventory management of malaria commodities, and EUV
		100,000	-	Zanzibar	

Proposed Activity	Mechanism	Budget		Geographic Area	Description
		Total $	Commodity $		
Subtotal Pharmaceutical Management		**850,000**	-		
SUBTOTAL CASE MANAGEMENT		**10,082,300**	**4,800,000**		
HEALTH SYSTEM STRENGTHENING / CAPACITY BUILDING					
Capacity building	NMCP	150,000	-	Mainland	Support for capacity building for the NMCP. This includes in-house trainings, attendance at conferences, health promotion unit, and study tours
	ZAMEP	110,000	-	Zanzibar	Support for capacity building for the NMCP. This includes in-house trainings, attendance at conferences and study tours
Peace Corps	Peace Corps	40,000	-	Nationwide	Support for three Peace Corps Volunteers
Continued support to FELTP	CDC	150,000	-	Nationwide	Support to FELTP trainees with focus on malaria
Finance, HRH, Governance HSS national and LGA level	PS3	450,000	-	Mainland	Contribute to a project that will holistically address systems issues associated with the building blocks of human resources for health, governance, finance and information use
Results-based Financing (RBF)	World Bank	683,000	-	Mainland	Contribute to government-wide RBF scheme to improve the quantity and quality of health services including malaria

Proposed Activity	Mechanism	Budget		Geographic Area	Description
		Total $	Commodity $		
					prevention and case management, and availability of malaria commodities at health facilities
eLMIS phone application to expand eLMIS to facilities	TBD	300,000	-	Mainland	Support the training component of the eLMIS application roll out to improve commodity availability at health facilities
Expert Committee to help ZAMEP move towards pre-elimination	ZAMEP	15,000	-	Zanzibar	Support a committee of malaria experts to help Zanzibar analyze and evaluate local data and give guidance on moving towards elimination
SUBTOTAL HSS & CAPACITY BUILDING		**1,898,000**	**0**		
BEHAVIOR CHANGE COMMUNICATION					
	TBD - BCC Mechanism	2,000,000	-	Mainland	BCC across all interventions including mass media such as radio, printed materials, community mobilization, supporting community (*shehias*) committees, advocacy, commemoration of Malaria Day (25 April)
BCC across all interventions	ZAMEP	235,000	-	Zanzibar	BCC across all interventions including mass media such as radio, printed materials, community mobilization, supporting community (*shehias*) committees, advocacy, targeted messages for

Proposed Activity	Mechanism	Budget		Geographic Area	Description
		Total $	Commodity $		
					coastal areas, commemoration of Malaria Day (25 April), and dissemination and BCC around malaria bylaws.
School Health Program	ZAMEP	26,000	-	Zanzibar	Support for supervision of 300 malaria school clubs which cover messages and sensitize of school kids and parents/local communities on malaria messaging (ITN, IRS campaigns, etc).
SUBTOTAL BCC		**2,261,000**	**0**		

MONITORING AND EVALUATION

Epidemic Surveillance and Response

Proposed Activity	Mechanism	Budget		Geographic Area	Description
		Total $	Commodity $		
Support of eIDSR	TBD - Surveillance Mechanism	500,000	-	Mainland	Support for continuation of eIDSR rollout in the 10 remaining regions
Maintain Malaria Early Epidemic Detection System (MEEDS) reporting and outbreak preparedness/ response	TBD - Surveillance Mechanism	222,000	-	Zanzibar	Operational costs for MEEDS reporting and outbreak response system including technical assistance and support for day-to-day operations, printing of reports
	ZAMEP	526,000	-	Zanzibar	Direct support to ZAMEP to oversee/supervise MEEDS network and the District outbreak response team including the IT component of the MEEDs system

Proposed Activity	Mechanism	Budget		Geographic Area	Description
		Total $	Commodity $		
Subtotal Epidemic Surveillance and Response		**1,248,000**	**0**		
M&E Support					
Routine System Strengthening	TBD - Surveillance Mechanism	200,000	-	Mainland	Support the RSS activity to improve malaria data quality and use within HMIS in order to monitor changes in malaria burden over time and inform program planning
Dissemination of findings of continuous net distribution evaluation	ZAMEP	12,000	-	Zanzibar	Feedback meeting with CD implementers and partners for the ITN continuous distribution
Malaria Indicator Survey (MIS)	ICF Macro	1,500,000	-	Nationwide	Support for the 2017-18 MIS. This survey will help to evaluate the 2015-2016 LLIN Replacement Campaign, will include malaria prevalence biomarkers and will provide critical outcome and impact data
Integrated supportive supervision	NMCP	150,000	-	Mainland	Integrated supportive supervision and verification of interventions and coordination of Technical Working Groups for all activities by NMCP (Ento, MIP, BCC, M&E...)
	ZAMEP	160,000	-	Zanzibar	Integrated supportive supervision and verification of interventions

Proposed Activity	Mechanism	Budget		Geographic Area	Description
		Total $	Commodity $		
					and coordination of Technical Working Groups for all activities by NMCP (Ento, MIP, BCC, M&E...). Also includes quarterly integrated visits for monitoring and supervision of RDTS, microscopy QA/QC, and surveillance
Program monitoring and project management support	TBD - Monitoring, Evaluation, and Learning Program	294,000	-	Nationwide	This project develops a Mission wide database for implementing partners to submit malaria data, assists implementing partners develop performance management plans, and conduct data quality assessments on key malaria indicators.
Technical assistance for M&E	CDC	20,000	-	Nationwide	Two TA visits to support strengthening of malaria surveillance and other monitoring activities
Subtotal M&E		**2,336,000**	**0**		
Entomological Monitoring					
National insecticide resistance & intensity monitoring; longitudinal monitoring and IRS bioefficacy in the Lake Zone	IRS 2 TO6 (AIRS)	650,000	-	Mainland	Support longitudinal monitoring in the Lake Region, insecticide resistance monitoring at 22 national sentinel sites, and WHO bioassays to monitor insecticide residual efficacy

Proposed Activity	Mechanism	Budget		Geographic Area	Description
		Total $	Commodity $		
Entomological monitoring QA for 62 sites	IRS 2 TO6 (AIRS)	100,000	-	Mainland	Support oversight costs for all activities from mosquito field collection, sample processing/analysis in the laboratory to data collection and information quality
Entomological and insecticide resistance monitoring including PCR	ZAMEP	236,000	40,000	Zanzibar	Support entomological sentinel surveillance sites including operational cost for PCR
Procurement of entomological supplies	CDC	10,000	-	Nationwide	Procurement of entomological supplies
Technical assistance entomological monitoring	CDC	43,500	-	Nationwide	3 TA visits to support entomological monitoring to NIMR Mwanza and Zanzibar to provide TA to increase ELISA capability for blood meal analysis
Subtotal Entomological monitoring		1,039,500	40,000		
SUBTOTAL M&E		4,623,500	40,000		
OPERATIONAL RESEARCH					
N/A		0	-		
SUBTOTAL OPERATIONAL RESEARCH		0	0		
IN-COUNTRY STAFFING AND ADMINISTRATION					

100

Proposed Activity	Mechanism	Budget		Geographic Area	Description
		Total $	Commodity $		
Staffing and administration	USAID	1,700,000	-	-	Support for salaries, benefits, and administration costs
	CDC	660,000	-	-	
SUBTOTAL IN-COUNTRY STAFFING		2,360,000	0		
GRAND TOTAL		45,000,000	13,945,000		